MYSTERIES
OF THE MIDDLE AGES

MYSTERIES OF THE MIDDLE AGES

TRUE STORIES FROM THE MEDIEVAL WORLD

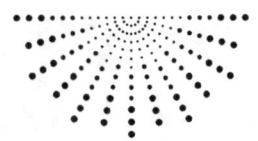

E.B. WHEELER

Rowan Ridge
Press

ISBN: 978-1-960033-04-8

First printing: June 2023

Published by Rowan Ridge Press, Utah

Cover and interior design © Rowan Ridge Press

Cover image by grandfailure via Deposit Photos

 Created with Vellum

CONTENTS

For everyone who wonders what happened back then

NOTE FROM THE AUTHOR

The stories in this book are true, based on the most reliable historical and modern sources I could find (you can see a list of the main sources for each chapter at the back of the book). Writing about the Middle Ages is tricky because fewer people then knew how to read and write—and many of them were too busy farming or fighting to keep records anyway. The people who did write down news and history weren't always eyewitnesses—they only wrote what other people told them, so they might not be accurate. And then those records had to survive hundreds of years of floods, fires, plagues, raids, wars, and page-munching pests to reach us. It's amazing we know anything about what happened in the past! We try to fill in the gaps with modern sciences like archeology, but the further you travel into the past, the more mysterious it becomes because there are so many things we don't know. Where possible, I used first-hand accounts to reconstruct these stories, but I often had to guess exactly what people said, did, and thought based on the information available.

"Middle Ages" and "Medieval" (which is Latin for "Middle Age" and has nothing to do with "evil" as people sometimes think) are terms from European history, referring to the time between the Classical world of Rome and the Renaissance, when discoveries in science, art, exploration, and printing began the modern world that we live in. People sometimes call them the European Dark Ages, and some things about the times were dark—for hundreds of years, Europeans went without important things like indoor plumbing and representation in government. But it was also a time of creativity and growth, and Medieval people had some skills that modern people are still trying to understand.

Though the term Middle Ages is European, this book has mysteries from other parts of the world as well. During the European Middle Ages, people all across the world were building great empires, unknowingly preparing for the catastrophic showdown at the beginning of the modern world when advances in science and travel would bring the world closer together. Islamic forces from the Middle East spread their control across parts of Asia, North Africa, and into Spain in Europe. The African continent saw the rise of several huge and wealthy empires such as Zimbabwe and Timbuktu. In China, the Tang, Song, and Ming dynasties flourished, giving us important inventions such as the printing press and gunpowder. This was the era of "Classical Japan," when the Yamato clan established the dynasty that still serves as the head of state for Japan to this day and gave rise to feudal Japan—the age of the samurai. In North America, the Mississippian culture, which built huge earthworks, thrived during the Middle Ages, and the Ancestral Puebloans built their villages in the cliffs of the American Southwest. Farther south in the Americas, the Mayan, Toltec, Aztec, and Incan cultures built amazing structures. All of these civilizations left behind mysteries for us to wonder about.

I hope you enjoy trying to solve each mystery and perhaps find one that sparks your curiosity to dive deeper into this part of history.

ICELAND

CANADA BRITISH GERMANY MONGOLIA
ISLES

UNITED
STATES

CONSTANTINOPLE CHINA JAPAN

MEXICO

EGYPT

MALI

PERU

POLYNESIA

EASTER
ISLAND

ZIMBABWE

1
KING ARTHUR

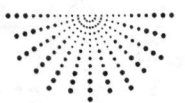

King Arthur might be the most famous—and most mysterious—figure from Medieval Europe. Stories say he pulled the sword Excalibur from a stone and sat at a round table with his knights and the wizard Merlin in Camelot. These are just legends, but King Arthur was a real person— maybe. Some historians say he never existed. Others say he was not only real but also helped shape the Middle Ages. Once you read the facts as we know them, you can decide what you believe. Either way, Arthur's stories rose from the ashes of a fallen empire, a symbol of a new age of the world.

In 400 AD, Rome ruled one of the largest empires the world had yet seen. The Roman Empire stretched across parts of Asia, Africa, and Europe. It united millions of people from Egypt to England with a common language, religion, and government. Rome was called the Eternal City. It had reigned supreme for nearly 800 years, suffering few serious military setbacks for centuries.

Rome ruled a huge Empire—perhaps too large to maintain. Note that the Scots lived in what is now called Ireland, and the Picts lived in modern Scotland. Both were enemies of the Roman Britons. Image courtesy of Furian via Deposit Photos.

All of that was about to change.

As the Roman poet Claudian said, "Men are raised high so they may fall more heavily." In other words, "The bigger they are, the harder they fall."

Rome's massive size meant it had a huge border to protect and a lot of neighbors who were tired of Rome pushing them around. The Romans called these people barbarians, basically "ignorant foreigners." But the barbarians were strong and ambitious. The Roman Empire had suffered from a series of weak and corrupt leaders. It didn't have the money to maintain such a large government and army and relied heavily on slave labor. The empire was top-heavy and crumbling. It would only take a few pushes to topple the whole thing.

Rome once had one of the greatest armies in the world. By the end of the Empire, it struggled to find loyal and disciplined soldiers. Photo courtesy of delkoo via Deposit Photos.

The struggling empire, trying to stay alive, divided itself into smaller districts with co-emperors. Some Roman generals thought they could do a better job running things than the politicians. They summoned their loyal soldiers to help them take over. This left parts of the empire defenseless. In 410, the barbarian Visigoths took advantage of this weakness and invaded and plundered Rome. The shock sent tremors through the empire. The Eternal City had fallen.

One of the places left without an army in this chaos was Britain. The Scots and Picts of modern Ireland and Scotland began plundering the British cities.

The Britons asked the government for help, saying, "The barbarians drive us to the sea; the sea throws us back on the barbarians: thus two modes of death await us, we are either slain or drowned."

But the Roman Empire had a new problem: the fearsome barbarian warrior king Attila the Hun had attacked. The Britons were on their own.

The Britons hired barbarian Saxons to protect their cities. It wasn't long before the Saxons decided that they didn't need to protect the Britons—they could just take the island for themselves. Along with the related Anglian people, they would become the English. The Anglo-Saxons turned on the Britons and drove them west, into the mountains of Wales (a word which comes from the Saxon word for "foreigner," so now the "ignorant foreigners" were calling the Roman Britons "Welsh," or foreigners in their own land).

The British monk and historian Gildas, writing shortly after these events, said, "Some therefore, of the miserable remnant, being taken in the mountains, were murdered in great numbers; others, constrained by famine, came and yielded themselves to be slaves forever to their foes, running the risk of being instantly slain." He described the stones of city walls and towers lying in ruined streets along with "fragments of human bodies." So many people died that there was no one left to bury the dead.

It looked as though the barbarian invaders would wipe the Britons from the earth. Many Britons thought it was the end of the world.

What would you do in such a situation? Find a secret place to live in the mountains? Serve the Saxons so they would spare your life? Flee overseas and take your chances with the fighting in the crumbling Roman Empire? Or something else?

When times are dark, it sometimes brings out the hero in people. And that's where the mystery of King Arthur begins. One man stood up against the impossible odds of the Saxon invasion. Gildas tells us about this man: "Ambrosius Aurelianus, a gentleman, who of all the Roman nation was then alone in the confusion of this troubled period by chance left alive. His parents, who for their merit were adorned with purple, had been slain in these same broils [battles]."

After 1,500 years, this is the only record we have of Ambrosius Aurelianus from close to his lifetime. Most other stories that mention him were written much later and seem to get their information from Gildas. If not for Gildas's work surviving, we probably wouldn't know Ambrosius existed. His parents were apparently Roman military leaders or nobility killed in the Saxon uprising. He somehow survived the invasions and grew up to rally the Britons against the Saxons. We don't know where he came from or how he survived the slaughter of the Britons. Maybe he hid in the mountains until he was ready to fight. Maybe his parents sent him away, but he returned to Britain to avenge his people.

We do know he was successful at uniting his people and became a great military leader. Gildas says, "After this, sometimes our countrymen, sometimes the enemy, won the field...until the year of the siege of Badon-hill, when took place also the last almost, though not the least slaughter of our cruel foes."

The siege of Badon-hill, also known as the Battle of

Mount Badon, took place in about 500 AD. There, the Britons defeated the Saxons so thoroughly that archeology tells us the Saxons abandoned many of their settlements. They fled the borders of Wales for at least a generation, leaving the surviving Britons in peace.

Ambrosius Aurelianus, wherever he came from, saved his people by bringing them together to defend themselves. He changed the course of history for the Britons and their neighbors. The Britons began the process that would define Europe in the Middle Ages. People united under the rule of warrior kings who were strong enough to protect them. They lived in or near forts (later castles) where they could plant crops, make clothes and tools, and raise families in peace.

So, what does this have to do with King Arthur?

Later stories about King Arthur say he led the victory at the Battle of Mount Badon.

The red dragon is the national symbol of Wales. It's supposed to be an emblem for Arthur, who was sometimes called by the name Pendragon or "head dragon." Image courtesy of Steve Allen via Deposit Photos.

The problem with Arthur's history is that Gildas doesn't mention him. No one who lived at that time did. The first records of Arthur came hundreds of years later. The monks who wrote his history mixed it with legends about dragons, a single warrior slaying a thousand men at once, and a dog so big he left paw prints in stone. These writers believed many fantastical things were possible, which makes it hard to trust their records.

Arthur might even be a nickname instead of a real name. It could come from the Roman name Artorius. Other historians think it comes from the old British word for bear, "arth," and was used to describe a leader who fought like a bear. Some even suggest that Arthur was an ancient Celtic bear god whose stories were mingled (or mangled) with history.

But starting around 600 in Wales, Scotland, and Ireland, the name Arthur suddenly became popular in noble families. This seems to show that the Celts were naming their sons after someone famous—like a war hero.

On the other hand, Celtic family histories don't show anyone named Arthur around the time of the Battle of Mount Badon. No one claimed him as an ancestor, and rulers in the past sometimes added heroes and gods to their family trees to make themselves look more important. So, what does that mean? Maybe everyone knew that Arthur didn't have surviving children (and therefore wasn't anyone's ancestor). Maybe his people called him by a different name. Or maybe he was only a story that gave people hope—like people naming their children after superheroes like Thor or Steve Rogers (Captain America).

Interestingly, even in ancient legends, Arthur either doesn't have children or only has one son, Mordred. In these stories, Mordred betrayed Arthur, and they killed each other in battle.

Arthur could have been a nickname for Ambrosius Aurelianus. Gildas doesn't make it clear if Ambrosius was the leader at the Battle of Mount Badon. If so, that would suggest that Ambrosius and Arthur are the same person. If this is true, however, Ambrosius lived and fought for a very long time. It was about fifty years between when the Saxons invaded and the Battle of Mount Badon. That's not impossible, but warriors in the early Middle Ages didn't often lead long lives. Also, Ambrosius was Roman, while later stories about Arthur focus on him as a Celtic war leader. And Gildas mentioned that Ambrosius had grandchildren alive at the time Gildas was writing. So, if Arthur was childless, he and Ambrosius are not the same person.

Ambrosius does make appearances in legends about King Arthur. In some stories, he is Arthur's uncle. In others, under the Welsh version of his name, Emrys, he is a wise man or magician who advises Arthur. This makes him similar to Merlin (who, you might be surprised to discover, was a real person—a poet or bard in the 500s called by the Welsh name Myrddin, though he was never known to perform magic, unfortunately). So, perhaps the real Arthur wasn't Ambrosius, but his protege, a literal or adopted heir to his leadership.

Arthur may also have been a competitor to Ambrosius. Perhaps he was a younger warrior who eventually took Ambrosius's position. Ambrosius's old Roman traditions gave way to Arthur's new British style of leadership.

A Medieval illustration shows Merlin or Emrys warning the British king Vortigern about the dragons fighting under his castle. Image courtesy of Wikimedia.

Some historians think this competition is why Gildas doesn't mention Arthur. He might have been a fan of Ambrosius and didn't want to give any credit to his hero's rival. Some later stories also said that Arthur humiliated Gildas's brother. These legends were written after Gildas's lifetime. If they're based on oral histories passed down over time, they might explain why Gildas didn't record Arthur's name and accomplishments.

Whatever Gildas's intentions, the stories of Arthur would not die. The Welsh and other Celtic people clung to his legends as they fought against the English for centuries. Arthur was their national hero—a fierce warrior and king capable of uniting his people and fighting giants and monsters. And the English and later Normans (from France) must have seemed like giants or monsters. Their much larger armies slowly gained more control over Welsh lands as the Welsh fought for their independence.

The English also stole Welsh stories. They transformed Arthur into an English king with French elements like

Lancelot and armored knights fighting in tournaments. The early Britons would not have recognized the King Arthur we know today.

King Arthur and his soldiers would not have worn heavy plate armor or jousted, both of which were later inventions.

If anyone else wrote about Ambrosius and Arthur close to their lifetimes, we've lost those records to time. We're only left with Gildas's short history. We're lucky it survived through all the centuries to offer us a hint about the chaos of the fall of Roman Britain and the man—or men—who helped save the Britons. One twist of fate, one ruined manuscript, and we might not know that Ambrosius Aurelianus was a real person. A different twist, and perhaps we could have had records telling us the truth about King Arthur. As it is, we can only enjoy the legends and try to guess about the real men behind them.

2
SECRET FIRE

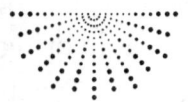

Constantinople was the last jewel in the crown of the Roman Empire. It was the largest and wealthiest city in Europe after Rome's decay. When the empire broke into smaller pieces, Constantinople stayed strong. It became the heart of the new Byzantine Empire. It sits between the Mediterranean and Black Seas as an important link between Europe and Asia. Its massive walls kept it safe from the barbarian invasions that wiped out most of the Roman Empire. It kept its own emperor after Medieval warrior kings like Arthur replaced Roman consuls.

In 678, however, it looked like Constantinople would fall to a different foe. Muslim forces swept north from Arabia. They conquered Egypt and Syria and chipped away at Constantinople's powers by land and sea. Finally, they surrounded the great city. The ringing of swords and the cries of soldiers echoed every day outside the walls. Enemy ships laid siege to the once-bustling harbor. It was only a matter of time until the great city of Constantinople fell to the highly organized Arab forces. Once the Muslim forces conquered Constantinople, the rest of the former Roman Empire would follow.

Refugees packed the streets of Constantinople. They had fled their own ruined cities for the one hope left of safety. Now, they huddled behind the great stone walls and wondered if the next day would bring their deaths.

One of these refugees, a Christian or Jewish architect named Kallinikos who had fled the Arabs in Syria, approached the emperor, Constantine IV. He had an idea.

"Your Highness," he said. "I have a secret that I think can save the city."

The shrieks and clashes of battle rolled over the massive walls of Constantinople.

"Tell me," the emperor said.

Emperor Constantine IV is the older man in the center of this Byzantine mosaic. Image courtesy of Wikimedia.

The greatest power of the Arab military in 678 was its navy. The Arab religious leader Muhammad ibn (son of) Abdullah founded the religion of Islam in 610. His followers, called Muslims, then united the tribes of Arabia. They stepped into the power vacuum left by the fall of the Roman Empire. They took control of the Middle East (the area around Arabia) and across North Africa to Spain. Now, the great Arab admiral Yazid ibn Shagara directed his ships in their siege outside the towering walls of Constantinople. Once the great city fell, the Arab armies could continue north, claiming more of the lands that had once been Rome's.

The walls of Constantinople protected the city for centuries.
Image courtesy of Bigdaddy1204 CC BY 3.0.

Some of the Jewish and Christian inhabitants of the Middle East had welcomed the Muslim conquerors. They were tired of being ruled by polytheists (believers in many gods) who placed extra taxes and rules on them for being monotheists (believers in one God). The Muslims were fellow "People of the Book." They followed the teachings of Abraham and Moses found in the *Bible* and the *Torah*. In many cases, they treated the Jews and Christians better than the previous rulers had. But Constantinople was already a Christian city. The Christians living there did not want to fall to foreign rulers.

After the collapse of the Roman Empire, the Byzantines

had fought off attacks by barbarian tribes from Europe. They also had to defend themselves from the mighty Persian Empire to the east. This had left their forces weak, like a boxer taking punch after punch, growing bruised and tired. Arab Admiral Yazid felt confident that his navy would deliver the blow that brought down the great Byzantine city.

The navy of Constantinople sailed out across the rippling blue waters to face Yazid's ships. They had to protect the city. If not, this would be the day that the Byzantine navy sunk to the bottom of the sea and Yazid took Constantinople.

Yazid ordered his ships forward. "Attack!"

The Arab ships adjusted their sails, and the oarsmen steered out to meet the Byzantine ships.

The Byzantine ships had changed a little since the Arab navy had last faced them. They now had long nozzles on the front of each ship. The Arab ships caught the wind and raced forward.

The sailors on the Byzantine ships worked a pump that sprayed liquid from the nozzles on their ships. The liquid hit the Arab ships. Then it burst into flame. The Arab sailors threw water on the fires to put them out. The water made the flames roar up like angry lions, consuming the sails and the decks of the wooden ships. Some of the burning liquid got onto the sailors. It stuck to them, searing their skin. They jumped into the water, but that didn't stop the fire. Instead, the flames burned on the water, turning the sea into a chaos of fire and screaming as Arab ships burned and sank.

Yazid had seen fire used in battle before, but never like this. The Byzantines had a terrible new weapon. Yazid didn't know how to fight it. He would lose his whole navy if he didn't do something.

"Retreat!" he called.

The surviving Arab ships hastily sailed away. They sailed right into a storm that further damaged the Arab navy, taking Yazid and many of his remaining forces to the sea floor. Kallinikos's secret had saved Constantinople.

A Medieval illustration of Greek fire at work. Image courtesy of Wikimedia.

Emperor Constantine had been desperate enough to try Kallinikos's new idea when the Arabs had his city under siege. The gamble paid off. Exactly what the emperor and the architect discussed remains a mystery to this day. Kallinikos's secret was so important that only the emperor was allowed to know it. No single craftsman built the new weapon. Each person worked on a different part so they wouldn't learn the weapon's secrets. Only Kallinikos and Constantine knew exactly how the whole thing fit together. They would only reveal the process to the next emperor. The new weapons turned the tide against the formidable Arab forces, who had conquered almost without pause since leaving Arabia.

The Arabs put their best chemists to work trying to copy

the formula. They came up with several ways to shoot flames, but never anything like Greek Fire. They also practiced putting wet leather on their boats and fighting in the rain, but none of these stopped the power of Constantinople's secret weapon.

For the next several hundred years, Constantinople used Greek Fire to protect itself from Arabs, Russians, Vikings, and even its neighbors to the west. The former Western Empire and the Byzantines were both Christian societies and heirs of Rome. Yet they followed different leaders and traditions, so they often fought each other. When knights from France and England set off on the Crusades to try to reclaim Jerusalem —a city holy to Jews, Christians, and Muslims—from the Arabs, they often took a swipe at Constantinople on their way. Greek Fire was Constantinople's best protection.

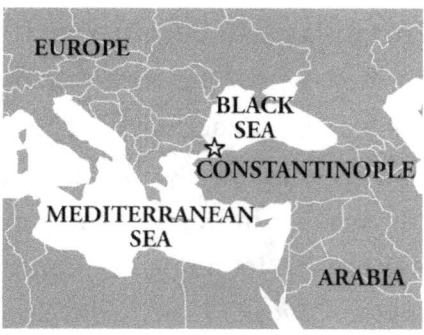

Sitting in an important position between Europe and the Middle East, Constantinople had to stand against enemies from both sides.

The problem with carefully guarded secrets is that if the wrong person dies, the knowledge can be lost forever. That seems to be what happened to Greek Fire. Many things about

Greek Fire are a mystery. We don't know exactly when the formula was forgotten, but at some point, the Byzantines lost their secret weapon.

The Byzantine princess Anna Komnene, born in 1083, was once first in line to inherit the throne of Constantinople. She probably knew more than most people about how Greek Fire worked—perhaps all of its secrets. But then her father Alexios died and her younger brother became emperor instead of her. She tried to take the throne from him and failed. Her brother banished her from the city in 1119. She spent much of the rest of her life writing about Constantinople's history.

She was about fifteen during the First Crusades when French knights attacked the city. Constantinople drove off the knights with Greek Fire. She described the preparations, "on the prow of each ship [Emperor Alexios] had a head fixed of a lion or other land-animal, made in brass or iron with the mouth open and then gilded over, so that their mere aspect was terrifying. And the fire which was to be directed against the enemy through tubes he made to pass through the mouths of the beasts, so that it seemed as if the lions and the other similar monsters were vomiting the fire."

A frightening and effective defense.

But in 1203, when the Fourth Crusade attacked Constantinople, there was no Greek Fire to protect them. The Crusaders raided the city and put a ruler they chose on the throne. It seems that sometime in the fifty years between Anna's death in 1153 and the Fourth Crusade, the secret of Greek Fire was lost. Maybe Anna herself had the formula and refused to pass it on to future rulers after she lost the throne. We'll never know what secrets she took to her grave.

Fire was still used in warfare, but it was not the famous Greek Fire. Another invention of the Middle Ages—this one from China—finally overcame Constantinople: gunpowder.

In 1453, the Muslim Turks of the Ottoman Empire laid siege to Constantinople. The Byzantines had faced plagues and wars and had forgotten the secret of Greek Fire. They had lost most of their armies, land, and power and had little left to defend themselves. Other Christian countries ignored their pleas for help. The Western European leaders didn't believe that the nineteen-year-old Ottoman Emperor, Mehmed II, posed any threat. But Mehmed II brought in huge cannons, including one that could fire a 600-pound stone ball. Under the onslaught, the great walls of Constantinople finally collapsed. The Ottoman Empire claimed Constantinople.

Constantinople finally fell to gunpowder weapons. Image courtesy of Wikimedia.

To this day, no one knows how the Byzantines made their "Greek Fire," but we have some guesses.

Anna Komnene mentioned that some generals used naphtha, pitch, and dry wood to start fires in battle. This wasn't Greek Fire—it was only used to burn wooden towers built by the enemy and wasn't shot from the mouths of brass animals—but it was effective in warfare. Naphtha can be made from several flammable oils. In Anna's time, it probably came from the petroleum found throughout the Middle East.

Pitch is similar to turpentine. It's a thick resin made from pine sap that was often used in the cracks of ships to make them waterproof. So, Anna was describing gasoline and perhaps turpentine used on the battlefield. Water doesn't put out a gasoline fire, and resin is sticky, which are two characteristics of Greek Fire, but these two alone don't seem to make Constantinople's Greek Fire.

Another ingredient that may have been part of Greek Fire was quicklime. Quicklime is calcium oxide: fine, white crystals formed when limestone is heated. It has long been used in making mortar to hold stones together, such as in the pyramids of Egypt, Roman aqueducts, and the Great Wall of China. When it's not mixed with other materials, though, quicklime has a property that made it effective and horrifying in warfare: when it gets wet, it becomes burning hot.

Jugs of quicklime thrown like grenades into the lines of enemy soldiers would float in the air in a cloud of fine, white powder. When it drifted into the eyes, noses, mouths, and lungs of soldiers, it burned and blinded them. Because liquid makes it hotter, some people think it was a part of Greek Fire. It might have helped to heat the other fuels in the weapon when it touched water. And Kallinikos, the inventor of Greek Fire, was an architect, so he was probably familiar with quicklime.

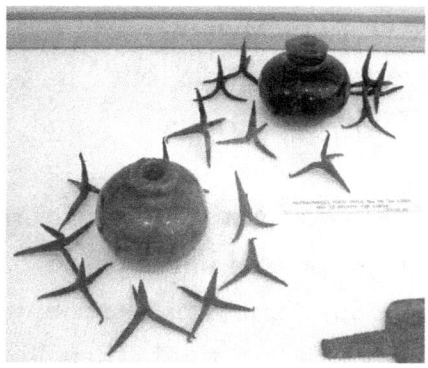

These Medieval grenades would have been filled with burning liquid—a weapon inspired by Greek Fire. Photo courtesy of Chania Badseed GNU 2.5.

Greek Fire would no longer be effective against the weapons in modern warfare, but that hasn't stopped people from trying to discover how the Byzantines did it. Chemists have created similar substances, but none exactly match the descriptions of Greek Fire, a formula lost to history.

3

THE SILENT SENTINELS OF THE RAPA NUI

On the most remote inhabited island in the world, the huge heads of giant stone statues stand with their backs to the sea. They look inward over the island, their eyes cold and empty. Elsewhere, scattered across the island, half-finished statues lie neglected in quarries. Others were dragged out of the quarry and then abandoned. We know who built the statues, but we don't know how or why—or why they stopped. Their descendants, the Rapa Nui, still live on the island, but none of them now can read the ancient writing that might tell the secrets of the statues. A brutal history has wiped out many of their stories. The statues and the story of the civilization that created it remain one of the most haunting mysteries of the Middle Ages.

Despite what we don't know about the early Rapa Nui and their statues, we have enough clues about their lives that we can piece together parts of a story about what might have happened on their island. Let's try to imagine the life of a young Rapa Nui during the time of the great statues based on what we have been able to learn about their culture.

During the Middle Ages, most peoples saw the oceans as a daunting barrier to travel or exploration—the unknown too terrifying and deadly to risk. The Vikings were one exception, but even they stayed fairly close to land. The Polynesian people of the Pacific Ocean, however, saw the waters as a great highway. With their canoes and their knowledge of the stars and the tides, they became the great seafarers of the Middle Ages. They ventured out thousands of miles from home to discover and settle new lands.

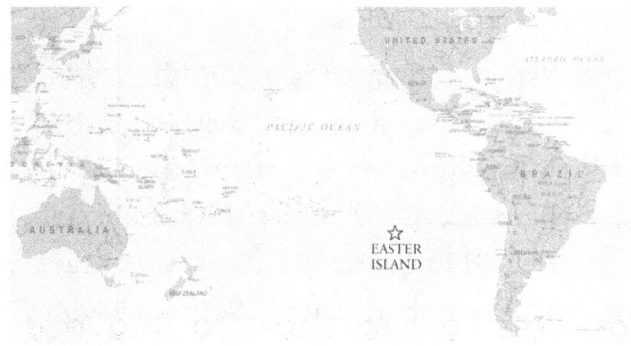

Rapa Nui, or Easter Island, is the most remote inhabited place in the world—a testament to the sailing and navigating skills of the Medieval Polynesian people. Image courtesy of dikobrazik via Deposit Photos.

The ancestors of our imagined Rapa Nui boy or girl were among these Polynesian explorers. Rapa Nui legends say their first king came to the island fleeing a terrible calamity like a war or tsunami. It must have been truly terrible to drive people to the island now called Easter Island. The island is 1,400 miles from the nearest continent, South

America, and over a thousand miles from the next inhabited island. Our young Rapa Nui would have known legends about what brought his or her ancestors to this remote island, but after several hundred years on the island, the stories might not have been close to the truth anymore.

Despite the great distance between the Rapa Nui and other people, they may not have been totally isolated. As a Polynesia people, the Rapa Nui came from the direction of Asia. They brought chickens with them to the island, and also bananas, both of which come from Southeast Asia. They did not have pigs or dogs like many other Polynesian people. Instead, their most important food was the sweet potato—a food from South America.

"We are born eating sweet potatoes, we die eating sweet potatoes, and in between, we eat many sweet potatoes," our young Rapa Nui's mother might remind them.

But how did the Rapa Nui get sweet potatoes? Did their ancestors sail to South America before settling on Rapa Nui? Or did they travel the incredible distances across the ocean to trade? Our young Rapa Nui might know the answers, but we don't.

So, our Rapa Nui friend no doubt spent part of the day tending sweet potatoes, harvesting bananas, and gathering chicken eggs. If he was a boy, he might also climb the cliffs to gather the eggs of sea birds nesting there. He could also venture out in a canoe to fish for spiny lobster or tuna—the tuna being a treat reserved only for members of royalty. The Rapa Nui loved to throw huge feasts and made sure that any leftover food went to hungry family members.

Another part of a young Rapa Nui's day was probably

spent combating the Rapa Nui's worst enemy: rats. The rats came as stowaways either with the first settlers or later traders. They weren't native to the island and didn't have any natural predators there. The Rapa Nui didn't have cats or dogs, so they had no animals to keep the rats in check. A female rat can have six litters a year of up to twelve rats at a time, which means a single pair of rats can have over 1,000 descendants in one year. If allowed to reproduce unchecked, that multiplies to half a billion rats in three years.

Considering there were probably only around 15,000 Rapa Nui people at the population's height, it would have been a never-ending battle to keep the rats from overwhelming the island. The Rapa Nui constantly fought the rats, who ate their crops and the seeds of the giant palm trees that once dominated the island. Our young Rapa Nui probably had to eat rat meat often. It was not a favorite food—the royalty refused to eat rats, claiming it would sully their royal powers and make the chickens stop laying eggs.

Despite these struggles to survive, the Rapa Nui still had time to build. Our young Rapa Nui lived in a stone house and kept his or her chickens in a stone coop. And then there were the stone statues—the moai. The "Easter Island heads" are world famous, but how did they look to the people who built them?

For our Rapa Nui, the moai weren't just heads. The heads of the statues are extra large, but they have a body as well and sit on a platform. They may represent ancestors or past rulers. Some of them are even painted. They didn't stare out to the ocean as we often imagine, but faced inward, watching the villages. That might have been reassuring if they were considered guardians, but we don't know how the Rapa Nui felt about them at the time. The moai could have been threatening—like the statues were spying on them for the rulers, making sure everyone stayed in line.

These moai are restored to their original positions, with their full bodies visible and their backs to the sea. Photo courtesy of OlyPhotoStories via Deposit Photos.

Many of the Rapa Nui must have been involved in creating and moving the moai whether they wanted to be or not. The moai were carved out of relatively soft volcanic rock in a quarry on one side of the island. On average, they are thirteen feet tall—about the height of a single-story house. Most weigh about fourteen tons or as much as two school buses. The largest weigh over 80 tons and are as tall as a three-story building. Special craftsmen carved the moai, but many more people must have been involved in moving the huge statues and placing them on their platforms.

Moving the huge moai would have been a monumental task. Photo courtesy of VladimirKrupenkin via Deposit Photos.

There are two ways our young Rapa Nui might have helped move the moai. One is they might have cut down some of the huge palm trees on the island to make rails or logs for rolling the statues along. Some of the old legends about the Rapa Nui kings say that they commanded the statues to walk. Modern people have wondered if the statues were "walked" into place by rocking them back and forth, and they have proven it could have been done. But we don't know for certain.

We do know it would have been a huge amount of work to move the moai. The task was likely overseen by the royal and priest classes while the common working people of the island did the hard work. So, unless our young Rapa Nui was royal, he or she may have taken time away from the battle against the rats to help haul the massive statues across the island.

The strangest thing about the moai isn't that the Rapa

Nui made the statues—many people create grand memorials representing leaders or religious figures—it's that they stopped so suddenly. Half-finished moai linger in the quarry centuries after they were begun. Completed moai lie abandoned along the route to their destinations. What made the people desert the moai and never try to finish them?

We can only guess what our imagined Rapa Nui experienced. Maybe a great natural disaster such as a volcanic eruption or earthquake frightened the people into giving up the moai. Maybe the people rebelled against being forced to move the statues while rats attacked their crops and chicken coops. We know the island's palm trees went extinct through a combination of humans cutting them down and rats eating their seeds so new trees never grew. Maybe without the tree trunks, the Rapa Nui could no longer move the statues. The people didn't attack the statues, as they might have done if they blamed them for their troubles, but it's as if they stopped caring about them.

The giant palm trees that once covered Easter Island are now extinct, leaving it bare of trees and more exposed to the ocean winds. Photo courtesy of abriendomundo via Deposit Photos.

The end of the moai was only one part of the Rapa Nui's

troubles. Later stories tell tales of wars between clans, and even of cannibalism—perhaps a sign of starvation. We don't know what our young Rapa Nui would have suffered or if he or she would have survived the wars.

Some of the Rapa Nui could write—probably the royalty or the priests—and we have the carvings of their language, which are called Rongorongo, which means "chanting." This suggests the language had a ritual or religious component. The writing is found all over the island on wooden plates, on walls, and even on the statues. But no one is left who remembers how to read the writing that might tell us more about the fate of the Rapa Nui.

An example of Rongorongo. No one can now read this language. Image courtesy of Wikimedia.

On Easter Day of 1722, when European explorers reached the island and gave it its modern name of Easter Island, there were only a few thousand Rapa Nui left. Outside records of the island are decades apart since it's so remote that foreigners rarely visited. The records visitors did keep show a population dwindling further. At one point, a slave raid took many Rapa Nui away, and when some of them returned, they brought outside diseases with them. By 1877, only 111 native Rapa Nui still lived on the island. They could not read their ancestor's language, and the violence of the previous century had stripped much of their culture and heritage from them.

Also, during this time, the moai had toppled over. We don't know why this happened—if it was due to natural disasters or if the people themselves knocked the statues down. Most of the moai were upright when the Europeans first visited, but by the end of the 1800s, none of them remained standing. The island is volcanic and has earthquakes, but it's strange that all the statues fell over in the 150 years after the first Europeans arrived. If the surviving Rapa Nui knew why, they didn't share the details with outsiders. They hinted at earthquakes and fighting among the clans. Some legends say a Rapa Nui priest or magical woman made the moai fall out of revenge when the people didn't share their food.

The South American nation of Chile later took over Easter Island. Its government raised a few of the moai and moved them to a position facing the sea. Later, the remaining Rapa Nui and foreign archeologists restored other moai in their original positions. But we still don't know why the Rapa Nui built the statues and what happened to their civilization once they did.

4
THE GREEN CHILDREN IN THE WOLF PIT

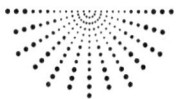

It sounds too strange to be true: sometime in the 1100s, a young boy and girl in odd clothes were discovered in a wolf pit in England. Strangest of all, the two siblings had green skin. They spoke a language no one understood. They refused to eat bread, meat, vegetables, or anything else until they spotted some broad beans and scarfed them down raw. As they tried other foods, their skin lost its green color. The children slowly learned English and told the villagers they came from another land where it was always twilight. The villagers had both children baptized, and the boy died. The girl lived out her life with the villagers, though she had a reputation for being stubborn and wild.

It's so outlandish that we might think it's just a strange folktale. Yet many people at the time believed and shared the story of the green children. Modern science and history offer a few explanations for who these children might have been —if they were real.

Wolves were still a serious threat to European villagers in the Middle Ages. Photo courtesy of VolodymyrBur via Deposit Photos.

The town of Woolpit is in the east of England. Its name comes from the wolf pits that were common there for trapping the wild wolves that still terrorized English farmers in the Middle Ages. There were at least two abbeys or monasteries nearby. This is significant because the monks who lived in these religious houses were some of the few people who could read or write at the time. The stories they recorded are our main sources for English history. Two monks with connections to the area, William of Newburgh and Ralph of Coggeshall, wrote versions of the story of the green children.

Books in the Middle Ages were written entirely by hand on very expensive parchment. This meant that monks only recorded things that they considered both true and important. Their standards were different from ours, though. Without telephones, the internet, or even newspapers, they couldn't always verify facts, although Willliam of Newburgh, in particular, tried to be accurate. The kinds of things they considered reasonable might seem strange to many modern people. This was a time before people understood germs or knew that the earth moves around the sun, governed by the laws of physics. Without modern medicine like antibiotics and painkillers, life was often short and painful.

People from every time and place want to understand why things happen. Medieval people often looked to the unseen, spiritual world for explanations. They were more likely than a modern person to believe in fairies, ghosts, and monsters. This doesn't mean they were stupid. They survived in a dangerous world that didn't have the benefits of scientific discovery that we enjoy now, and they were using the tools they had to understand the world. So, even William of Newburgh, with his concern about accuracy, wrote about things like revenants—reanimated corpses similar to vampires.

Medieval monks generally tried to record what they believed
to be true, but they made mistakes and sometimes gave into
their imaginations, like in this illustration of a wolf snail.
Image courtesy of Wikimedia.

Since monks might write about fantastical events that they considered warnings or miracles, could William's and Ralph's accounts of the green children be nothing more than a popular twelfth-century folk tale? The Medieval version of an urban legend?

There are some hints in the story that the green children might be connected to the world of the Faerie. These Faerie are not the little winged creatures of modern cartoons, but the old Fair Folk. Medieval Europeans believed there were small or human-sized persons who lived in an alternate land and had strange and dangerous powers. In some versions of the green children's story, they came through a cave, drawn by the sound of church bells. The world of the Fair Folk was supposed to be reached through a cave or underground passage. The Fair Folk are often associated with the dead, and there is evidence of that in the tale of the green children. Beans like those the children ate were considered a food of the dead in some folk stories. Plus, the children came from a land that's always twilight—neither day nor night. That could be a Faerie world or the land of the dead.

Why would the monks have carefully handwritten a fairy story in their histories of England? They might have believed that the Fair Folk were real and that England needed to be on guard against them. The monks may have seen the Faerie as a dangerous but less "advanced" race. After all, the boy died after being baptized and brought fully into the world of the Christian village, and the girl remained wild even after her baptism. Or, the monks may have felt there was deeper truth in this story because it showed the journey of humans from darkness to light, from past to present. The children were drawn from a twilight world by the songs of church bells.

Though it would be easy to write this strange story off as an old tale with only symbolic meaning, that may not be entirely true. After all, the story was written at about the same time by two people in different places who told slightly different versions of it. The differences in the story might seem like evidence against it, but they could actually support the story. It means the writers heard their information from two different sources. Many people had stories about the green children.

Monks had to write all of their records by hand. This monk drew a picture of himself at work. Image courtesy of Wikimedia.

When looking at history, it's always good to ask questions. Where did the writers find their information? Are those sources trustworthy? Who benefits from telling the stories?

Neither William nor Ralph claimed to have seen the green children themselves. First-hand evidence like that would have been the strongest. But Ralph said he heard the story from one of the men who personally helped rescue and raise the children, a man named Richard de Calne. Furthermore, Ralph's monastery was close to the village where the children were found. He said the girl had married someone in the village and died shortly before he was writing. So, his account wasn't based on a story that had passed through many people and changed over many years. He had personally interviewed people who had seen the children. William lived further from the village, but he knew monks in the area who could have told him the story.

If the people of Woolpit told the truth, and they did find two strange children with green skin in their wolf pit, how can we explain them?

The children's unusual clothing, speech, and eating habits have at least one reasonable explanation. The children might have been from another country and somehow become lost in England. At this time, few people ever left the village where they were born. So, even people who lived in the same country might seem foreign to each other.

Given their description of coming from a land always in twilight, maybe the children were from one of the countries farther to the north, like Iceland or Norway. In these countries near the Arctic Circle, the sun doesn't rise much beyond the horizon for months at a time. Think back to your earliest memories. How much of your home can you picture? Probably only one or two images that stuck in your memory. We don't know the exact ages of the children, but if they were young, the twilight months might have been all they could remember of their homeland.

Some people have also suggested the children might have been Flemish (from Flanders in what is now Belgium). There was a Flemish settlement not far from Woolpit, and there had recently been violence against Flemish immigrants after Flemish mercenaries fought on English soil. So, maybe the children had come with the families of Flemish mercenaries or weavers, and their parents had been killed. Then, the orphaned children wandered or hid until they found sympathetic villagers. The "twilight land" might have been a cave they hid in until fear, confusion, or hunger drove them to wander into the wolf pit.

So, there are possible explanations for the foreign nature of the children, but what about their green skin? Certainly, that's too fantastical to be true.

Maybe not. People with a very poor diet or certain infections can develop chlorosis or "green sickness." It's a form of anemia (lack of iron) that can cause sufferers to become pale and have a greenish tint to their skin. It's very rare today, with most people eating a healthier diet and having better access to medicines than in the past. Interestingly, old accounts of green sickness said it also caused a lack of interest in food. That fits with the children, whose green color went away as they eventually ate the food the villagers offered them. But if green sickness was more common in the past, wouldn't the people of Woolpit have seen it before? Is it possible that these children just had an especially severe case? Perhaps. And perhaps people's imagination or storytelling exaggerated how green the children were.

The broad beans mentioned in the story suggest another possible solution to the mystery. Some people have genetic "favism," an intolerance of fava and broad beans. The reaction is worse when the beans are raw. Their body's inability to digest these beans can cause confusion and jaundice. Jaundice normally gives skin a yellow tone, but in severe cases, it can also look green. And favism is more common and more severe in males. That could explain why the boy died and the girl survived. The main question unanswered by this theory is why the children would only eat broad beans—the food that was killing them.

The story of the Green Children of Woolpit continued to capture the English imagination long after the 1100s. In the 1600s, an Oxford scholar guessed that the children fell from "the heavens." An English bishop suggested that the children were extraterrestrial aliens in his book, *The Man in the Moone*. It was one of the first science fiction stories ever written.

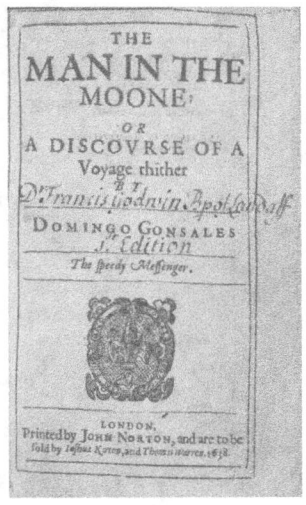

The green children of Woolpit inspired this early science fiction story. Photo courtesy of Harvard.

Is it possible that the green children were extraterrestrial aliens? "Little green men" are a staple of UFO stories. If the children's skin was green because of diet or some condition of their home planet, then living on Earth might have eventually turned them more human. It's unlikely that an alien species would look exactly like humans, though. And even less likely that they would marry and have children with humans, though some people in Woolpit claimed to be descended from the green girl.

But remember that William and Ralph were educated men who believed more in vampires and ghosts than germs and physics. Like them, there are some things we still don't understand about our world. Maybe in the future, we'll learn new things that will help explain the mystery of the Green Children of Woolpit.

5

LOST TREASURE OF THE STEPPES

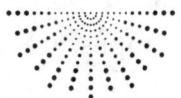

Somewhere in central Asia, perhaps in Mongolia or China, a lost tomb contains the remains of one man. His grave bears no markings. The cold winds sweep over it, whistling through the steppe grasses. The man in this forgotten tomb was once the most powerful person on earth. He is the ancestor of millions of people alive today. His memory was so strong that for a time, his people's enemies forbade anyone from speaking his name.

Along with the remains of this lone man may rest a fantastic treasure gathered from across much of the Eurasian continent. But the location of this grave has long been a mystery, and the treasure is lost to us.

The lost tomb—and its treasure—belong to a Mongolian man born in about 1162 named Temujin. His name means "made of iron" or "iron worker." When Temujin was born, there were many powerful empires surrounding the Mongols. The Muslim rulers of the Middle East had recently defeated the European armies of the Second Crusade. The Russians had established their base around the city of Kyiv on the eastern frontiers of Europe. The Jin Dynasty (family of rulers) in China was reaching the height of its power, extending the Great Wall and its control over neighboring states.

Between these Medieval powers were the steppes of Europe and Asia. The steppes are an enormous grassland populated by nomadic people who traveled around their territory, including the Mongols. These people had for many generations lived in clans or tribes based on family connections. Their life centered on raising horses and cattle. They were not only excellent riders but also expert archers. Their ability to shoot powerful bows while galloping their horses made them fearsome warriors.

The Mongols developed their riding and fighting skills living on the harsh steppes of Central Asia. Photo courtesy of brokenrecords via Deposit Photos.

Mongols often connected their clans through marriage.

When Temujin was nine, his father, the chief of his clan, arranged for Temujin to marry a girl named Borte from a neighboring tribe. This would solidify an alliance between their people. Nine was too young to marry, but Temujin's father sent him to live with his future wife's family until they were old enough to join their clans.

While Temujin was away, enemies poisoned his father. Despite his young age, Temujin returned to claim his role as chieftain. The clan rejected Temujin's claim. They abandoned Temujin, his mother Hoelen, and the rest of their family to survive on their own. Hoelen had been the chieftain's first wife—a politician and a warrior. She taught her children how to survive by gathering food, hunting, and fishing.

Being without a clan was dangerous. An enemy tribe captured Temujin at age fifteen and made him a slave. Temujin rebelled and escaped his captors. Legend says that one of the enemy soldiers was so impressed by Temujin's bravery that he let him ride away.

Temujin decided to honor the alliance his father made and returned to marry Borte. He established a household with his new wife, his mother, and his siblings. Soon after, a rival clan kidnapped Borte.

Temujin organized a rescue party with some of his friends. They saved Borte and killed every man who had helped kidnap her. Other clans took notice of Temujin's skills as a warrior and leader. They wanted to be his allies. When enemies attacked him or his allies, he defeated them. His reputation as a leader grew, and more people followed him.

Unlike other Mongol leaders, he didn't just choose

leaders from among his upper-class family members. He also found commanders from members of the lower classes who showed wisdom or skill in battle. This upset some Mongols who preferred the old ways, but Temujin's fame and power continued to grow.

In one battle, someone shot Temujin with an arrow. His forces were still victorious, and he rounded up the defeated soldiers.

"Which of you was it who shot me?" he demanded.

The soldiers had heard the stories of Temujin's vengeance on his enemies, and they were frightened. No one spoke.

"Tell me who it was!" Temujin said.

Finally, in the quiet, one soldier stepped forward. "I was the one who shot you."

Temujin stared down the enemy soldier. "You are brave to speak up, and you fight well. If you will swear loyalty to me, I will make you one of my commanders."

The soldier agreed.

Temujin jokingly called the soldier "Jebe," which means "arrow," as a reminder of that first meeting. Jebe went on to be one of Temujin's greatest commanders.

Temujin was ruthless in wiping out those who defied him or broke treaties with him. If enemy tribes surrendered, though, he took them under his protection. Hoelen adopted children orphaned by her son's wars. She brought them into her family to create unity. Having multiple wives was common among the Mongols. Temujin installed Borte as his chief wife and an important advisor, he also married the daughters of other leaders to solidify alliances between their families. A shaman, or religious leader, proclaimed that the entire world had been given to Temujin. This made some of his allies jealous, but he defeated those who turned against him.

Finally, in 1206, Temujin called a great meeting of the Mongol clans. He proclaimed himself leader over all the Mongols—about a million people. He also took a new name and title: Genghis Khan, meaning Fierce Ruler or Great Ruler. He forbade Mongols from kidnapping women or taking other Mongols as slaves. He did away with some of the harsher punishments for enemies and criminals, such as boiling them alive. He introduced a system of writing to the Mongols and recorded their laws. This let him create an early postal system for delivering messages. He also enforced religious tolerance. Some people of the steppes were Buddhist, Muslim, or Christian like their neighbors to the east, south, and west, and Genghis Khan allowed them the freedom to worship as they chose. The infighting among the Mongols essentially stopped.

A modern statue commemorating Genghis Khan. Photo courtesy of Hecke06 via Deposit Photos.

This peace was good for the Mongols but bad for their

neighbors. Now that the Mongols were working together, they turned their attention to conquering other people. They pushed back against the Jin Dynasty of China, which had been conquering Mongol tribes. The Mongols established the Yuan Dynasty, which would eventually rule China. When Middle Eastern rulers didn't respect their treaties with the Mongols, Genghis Khan wiped out their kingdoms. Russian leaders sent aid to some of their trading partners on the steppes who didn't want to surrender to Genghis Khan. The Mongols responded by rampaging through Kyiv. Their attack shook the kingdom of the Rus and sent refugees flooding west into Europe. Genghis Khan ruled an area four times larger than the Roman Empire at its height. Some historians estimate that up to 40 million people died during Genghis Khan's wars, or about ten percent of everyone living in the world at that time.

The Mongols collected loot like gold, silver, and silk from all of their conquered enemies. They also spared the lives of craftsmen like smiths and glassmakers in enemy cities. This made Genghis Khan and his people extremely wealthy. Ironically, the result of their warfare was an era of peace and wealth across a vast stretch of Europe and Asia. They stabilized the Silk Road, allowing safer travel and trade between Europe and Asia.

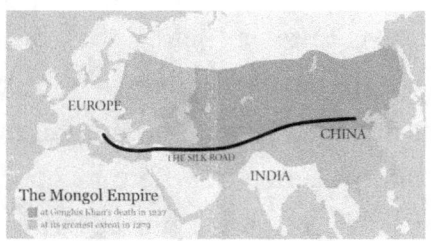

Genghis Khan and his successors took control of the Silk Road, allowing riches and ideas to travel from Asia to Europe. Image courtesy of Furian via Deposit Photos.

The Italian merchant Marco Polo journeyed along the Silk Road shortly after the reign of Genghis Khan. He brought tales of China's riches back to Europe. The skills of making gunpowder and printing books spread from Asia to Europe, which helped initiate the Renaissance and Age of Exploration in Europe. Foods like pasta and other new ideas traveled along the Silk Road along with wealth.

Unfortunately, this also spread the Black Plague as people exchanged goods (and germs) and refugees fled from the Mongols. The Black Plague or Black Death was the most deadly pandemic in history. The disease spread by the bites of fleas and sometimes by the coughs of infected people. It killed 100 million people or more in the Middle Ages.

Genghis Khan was a rich and powerful man by the 1220s. He maintained his nomadic lifestyle, traveling with soldiers, advisors, servants, tents, and treasure. When his children and grandchildren later created the capital city of Khara Korum, or "Black Tent," they wore golden jewelry, drank from a silver fountain shaped like a tree, used Chinese pottery, enjoyed Egyptian art, and collected gold and silver coins from all across Eurasia. Before they built their capital, these treasures would have traveled with them.

The greatest mystery about Genghis Khan surrounds his death. We don't know when or where he died, where he was buried, or what treasures were buried with him. This was intentional. Genghis Khan probably died sometime during the Mongols' war against the Western Xia Empire in China in 1227. He wanted his death to be secret so it didn't crush his soldier's morale or embolden his enemies. He would have been in his 60s during this war, which was old for the time. Yet he was still actively involved in fighting for and ruling his empire.

The Great Wall of China was extended to stop the Mongols, but it failed to hold them back. Photo courtesy of liushengfilm via Deposit Photos.

Some people think Genghis Khan died of a hunting injury or a wound sustained in battle. He also may have died of an illness like the Black Plague. A more colorful story says that a Chinese princess who was supposed to become one of his wives instead stabbed him to death. Either way, his family and advisors hid his death.

They also respected his wish to be buried in secret. Legend says that the soldiers accompanying his body to the burial place killed everyone they met on the way to keep their direction hidden. Then they rode horses over the gravesite to disguise its location. Some stories say Genghis Khan was buried in the mountains of modern Mongolia where he had hidden from his enemies as a young man. That region is vast and mostly empty of people, making it difficult to even guess where his tomb might be.

Historians can only speculate about what Genghis Khan's tomb is like, but we do have intriguing clues. Earlier rulers from the steppes were buried deep underground in chambers made with logs. Those chambers were filled with treasure from across Europe and Asia. These kings had nowhere near the wealth or power of Genghis Khan. His tomb is very likely a trove of wealth and information about the past. But so far, the steppes he once ruled have respected his final wish and kept his burial hidden from the world.

6

THE FORGOTTEN CITY OF THE MISSISSIPPI

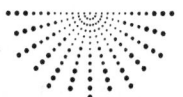

Imagine a huge city—one of the largest in the world during the Middle Ages. Its broad streets line up perfectly with the paths of the sun and the moon. High walls of huge wooden logs protect the inhabitants, who live in wooden houses with connecting courtyards. Outsiders walk hundreds of miles to trade and worship in the city. The streets echo with the voices of people bartering over deer, fish, and jewelry. Women chat as they weave cloth, and metal smiths hammer out copper jewelry. The scent of roasting corn and cooking fires fills the air. At the center of this great city rises a huge pyramid covering 14 acres—bigger than 10 American football fields and about ten stories tall.

This city might sound like something built by the Egyptians or the Aztecs in Mexico, but it's found in what is now Illinois in the United States, along the Mississippi River. Today, it's called Cahokia after the Native people who lived near it when the Europeans arrived. We don't know what its inhabitants called it. They didn't leave behind any writing, and their descendants told no stories about the city. It seems that, after Cahokia's fall, all the surrounding peoples were quick to forget about it. They didn't just forget about it but refused to talk about it and tried to erase it from their memories. Almost everything about Cahokia is a mystery.

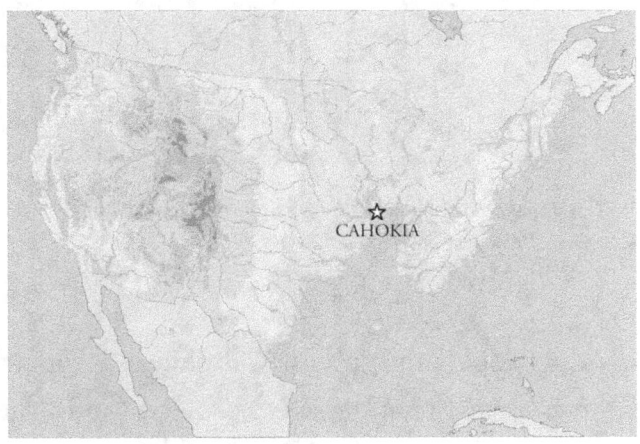

Cahokia's location along the Mississippi River. Image courtesy of delpieroo via Deposit Photos.

Cahokia arose from the Mississippian Culture. This was a Native American culture along the Mississippi River and in the eastern United States. It was known for building mounds of earth. Sometimes these mounds were used as platforms for building houses and sometimes for decorative or religious purposes. The people lived in villages ruled by chiefs. Their main crop was corn. They grew enough of it that not everyone had to spend their time farming. This meant they could have artists who created ceramics and jewelry. They sometimes hammered copper into decorative shapes and liked using shells to decorate their art and jewelry. They played sports, including an early version of lacrosse, which was invented by Native Americans. Some of the people belonging to this culture probably built the giant earth pyramids of Cahokia sometime around 1000 AD.

A panther vase from the Mississippian Culture. Photo courtesy of Madman2001 CC BY-SA 3.0.

The first strange thing about Cahokia is its location on the Mississippi River. Though rivers provide food, water, and transportation for cities, this portion of the Mississippi flooded often. That makes it a bad place for a large city. Some people had lived in the area before Cahokia. They must have known it wasn't an ideal place for a large city, but Cahokia's founders built there anyway. It was a planned city, with each street laid out according to a purpose. What the purpose was, though, and who designed the city, we can only guess.

Whatever the reason people built Cahokia, it was a back-breaking job. The great earthen mounds in the city took thousands of hours of work. People had to carry woven baskets full of dirt one load at a time to create the huge earthen pyramids. Why would people go to so much trouble to build something in a place where it would be damaged by high waters and have to be rebuilt again and again? Perhaps the location had religious significance. Maybe a powerful dynasty of rulers took a liking to the place and wanted to build there regardless of the risks. But the leaders were probably not the ones who carried all those baskets of dirt. Were the common workers volunteers, excited to be part of this massive project that would last a thousand years or more? Or were the leaders somehow forcing or frightening them into doing the work?

A reconstruction of how Cahokia looked at its height. Creating such a large city took thousands of hours of work. Image courtesy of Herb Roe CC BY-SA 4.0.

Because no Native American stories preserve the memory of Cahokia, archeology is our only key to understanding what happened there. That's how we know what the people ate, what their houses were like, and what kind of jewelry and pottery they used. For instance, we know they ate corn, used woven baskets, wore beaded jewelry, and carved small statues of women.

Early European explorers and settlers argued that the

Native people didn't tell stories about Cahokia because they didn't build it. They didn't believe (or didn't want to believe) that the Native people they were fighting could create great cities. They suggested instead that lost Egyptians or some other culture had settled there. Archeology puts that idea to rest. Analysis of the bones and teeth at Cahokia shows that the people of Cahokia were from the Mississippi River region and the eastern United States. We don't know if they came to trade, to worship, or even as tourists, but we know they were from North America.

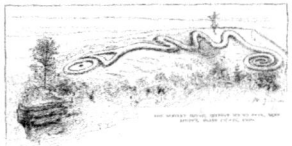

Other Native American groups built large earthworks such as the Serpent Mound in Ohio, but none built anything as massive as Cahokia. Image courtesy of Wikimedia.

Archeology also tells us that no major battles took place at Cahokia. Other Native sites in the region have remnants of arrowheads and other signs of war, but there are none at Cahokia. The people of the city enjoyed peace and prosperity —except for those who became human sacrifices, that is. Even though there are no signs of attacks on the city, it appears that Cahokia's leaders often reinforced their defenses, making the walls stronger. They weren't fighting anyone, but they were afraid of something.

The most strange and disturbing finds from Cahokia are those of Mound 72. This mound is just south of the largest pyramid in Cahokia. It's smaller than many of the other mounds, and it's lined up differently than the others. Most significantly, it contains hundreds of bones.

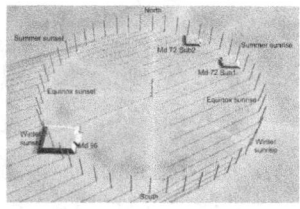

Mound 72's burials were topped with a "woodhenge" or circle of poles marking the solstices and other important astronomical events. Image courtesy of Herb Roe CC BY-SA 3.0.

Mound 72 holds what's called the "Beaded Burial." This is a collection of several bodies that were covered with beads made of seashells after they were buried. The two bodies in the center are a man and a woman. They're surrounded by the bones of several other men and women and even a child. They might have been an important family, but so far, analysis of the bones can't tell us anything more.

A disturbing twist on the Beaded Burial is that the other bodies found in Mound 72 are in mass graves. They appear to be human sacrifices. Most of them are teenage girls and young women, probably strangled to death. In one mass grave, there is a layer of bodies that were tossed in without any order and then topped by another layer of bodies that were placed carefully with wooden litters. Maybe these were nobility laid to rest on the bones of their enemies or servants? Analysis of the sacrifice victims' teeth shows that most of them came from Cahokia. Taken with the small statues of women found at Cahokia, it seems likely that the girls were sacrificed for religious reasons. We can only guess the reason for the sacrifices and the strange burials.

One of the last mass graves in Mound 72 is different. The people buried in it died violently. Their bones show marks from axes or clubs. Most of them are male, and they may be related to each other. Perhaps they were a group or family that rose in rebellion against the city or its rulers. This burial seems to mark the beginning of the end for Cahokia.

Cahokia's fall is just as mysterious as its rise. In about 1350, the city's social structure seems to have collapsed. People left the huge city, abandoning their homes. Some historians have wondered if the city's bad location finally caught up with it and a flood or other natural disaster destroyed the city. Recent archeology has disproven this idea, though. The layers of soil around Cahokia from that era are undisturbed. They show no sign of a cataclysmic flood, earthquake, or other disaster.

Perhaps the ruling family died off or something happened to shake the people's faith in the religion that brought them to Cahokia. Maybe they grew tired of the sacrifices they had tolerated for so long. Maybe those men who were buried in Mound 72 led some kind of revolt. Though they died, their rebellion may have kicked off a series of uprisings. But what would trigger such a violent change after people had been seemingly content at Cahokia for so long? Did the uprising weaken the ruling class, or perhaps expose weaknesses that had been there all along?

The largest pyramid mound at Cahokia today, now called Monk's Mound because it may have been used for religious ceremonies. Why would the people of Cahokia abandon their colossal earthen mounds and city? Photo courtesy of zrfphoto via Deposit Photos.

Cahokia is not the only ancient city of the Americas to be abandoned by its people. Teotihuacan was a great city in Mexico until about 600 AD. Something caused the people to rise up. They destroyed the religious symbols of their city and burned some of the buildings belonging to the ruling class. But people still lived on the outskirts of the city afterward. Later, other peoples came to visit and even worship there, calling it the "Place of the Gods." No such connection remained at Cahokia—everyone turned their backs on it.

Even the ancient cliff dwellings in the American Southwest were remembered after the builders abandoned them. The Navajo who later came to the area said they were built by the Anasazi or "ancient enemies."

But there are no stories of Cahokia. The city was not only forgotten but also erased from the memory of the neighboring peoples. It's as if they refused to even speak of the place. As if it was forbidden. When European explorers came up the Mississippi in the 1600s, none of the Native people could or would tell them anything about the city. Were the things that happened there so terrible that no one ever wanted to speak of them again? Whatever happened at Cahokia, it must have been terrible indeed for everyone to want to leave it in the past.

7
ALICE KYTELER: BLACK WIDOW, WITCH, OR WILY WOMAN?

Witch hunts were one of the darkest episodes of Medieval European history. It was a time when thousands of people who were different—who acted strangely, worshipped in their own way, or just didn't fit in with the right people—were hung or burned as witches. Many of these accused witches were women, though men were sometimes executed as well. Historians now view these so-called witches as victims of superstition and fear. They lived in an age when people constantly faced everything from warfare to plagues and were looking for people to blame or ways to regain control over their lives. But one of the earliest accused witches, an Irish woman named Alice Kyteler, may have actually been up to no good.

Alice was born in Ireland in the late 1200s. Unlike many later people accused of witchcraft, she came from a wealthy family. Her parents were part of the upper class made up of rich Flemish merchants and Norman-English nobility who invaded Ireland in the 1100s. The English nobility arrived after an Irish lord invited them to help fight his enemies, and then they turned on him (and if that doesn't sound familiar, reread the chapter on King Arthur).

Alice would have grown up learning to manage a household. That included running the kitchen and handling money. Like most Medieval girls, she was also expected to marry. She did all of these things well—perhaps a little too well.

First, she married a wealthy and well-connected banker named William Outlaw. Her age and the year she married William are unclear, but she was probably young. Some accounts say she married in 1280 at the age of seventeen. Marrying a wealthy man would have given her as comfortable a life as possible in an era without indoor plumbing, antibiotics, or the internet. She and William had one son, also named William Outlaw.

Kyteler Inn in Kilkenny, Ireland was supposed to have been founded by Alice Kyteler. Photo courtesy of littleny via Deposit Photos.

The elder William died. As was common for Medieval European widows, Alice continued managing his banking and money lending business. Her son joined her as a business partner when he was old enough. They were important people in Kilkenny, Ireland, wealthy and related to many of the ruling class. The younger William Outlaw even became mayor. It seems like they had things pretty good.

Medieval European widows had little incentive to marry again if they were wealthy. While she was a widow, a woman could own property and manage her own business. Once a woman married, her husband took control of everything she had. Legally, she ceased to exist as a person and became her husband's property.

Yet a wealthy widow with connections to the ruling class made an attractive wife. And two rich people who married could become even more powerful by joining their fortunes. So, Alice married again in 1302 to another wealthy banker and money lender named Adam le Blund. Medieval Europeans often married people in the same business as their family because they already knew how to succeed at the job. Weavers married weavers. Farmers married farmers. Bankers married bankers.

This pattern worked well for Alice. At one point, she and Adam had over 3,000 pounds in cash. This was a time when most people earned less than a couple of pennies a day, so maybe 6 pounds a year. In 1307, Adam signed his money and goods over to Alice's son William Outlaw. He did this even though he had children of his own from his first marriage. Adam died not long after.

This time, Alice didn't stay a widow for long. Within a couple of years, she married another wealthy widower and landowner named Richard de Valle. Richard didn't live for long after the marriage. When his son from his previous marriage refused to give the incredibly wealthy Alice her "widow's portion" of money, meant to keep widows from falling into poverty, she sued him. She wasn't letting a single penny slip away from her.

Medieval women could be money lenders, but people might envy their wealth and power. Image, "An Old Money-Lender," courtesy of the Prado Museum.

Her now-fatherless stepchildren became suspicious of her luck. She kept marrying rich men who died soon after and left her all their money. It looked like she might be a "black widow," killing a series of husbands.

This didn't stop a fourth widower from marrying her: Sir John le Poer. Alice now had money, land, and a title as the wife of a knight. Sir John became ill not long after their marriage. His hair fell out, and he grew thin and sickly. He told his adult children he suspected Alice was poisoning him. Poer's children talked with Alice's other stepchildren. They accused her of murdering her previous husbands. But they didn't stick to accusations of using poisons—a serious enough crime. They also said she had entranced her husbands with love spells (because apparently, her sacks of money weren't enough) and used witchcraft to make herself wealthy and kill their fathers.

The uproar engulfed Kilkenny. Alice was a powerful woman with a lot of friends, especially among the ruling class. Many of them did business with her, and quite a few were her relatives. They were not interested in seeing her tried for murder, even if her string of dead husbands was... suspiciously convenient for her.

Witchcraft was another matter, though. Many people practiced a kind of folk religion that blended ancient traditions and beliefs with Christianity. Most Catholic priests didn't like this, but they rarely bothered interfering as long as people still showed up at church. But the new local bishop, Richard de Ledrede, happened to be terrified of dark magic. He was certain that witches or sorcerers were out to get him. Many modern people think such a fear sounds silly. Yet Ledrede lived in an age when people didn't know about germs and had few medicines to treat pain and illness. Life seemed strange and uncertain to them, with death waiting just a whiff of foul air away. People tried to explain sudden deaths and bad luck in ways that made sense to them. For Ledrede, that way was the unseen forces of religion and its opponent, dark magic.

The local government wasn't interested in investigating the deaths of Alice's husbands, but Bishop Ledrede was. At this time in Europe, there were two sets of laws: the laws of kings and lords, and the laws of the Catholic Church. The king's law dealt with accusations of murder. The church's law investigated accusations of witchcraft since it was defined as having dealings with the devil.

We don't know if Alice's stepchildren really thought she was a witch or if they knew the bishop would take their side. Either way, they started one of the earliest witch hunts in Ireland. Bishop Ledrede accused Alice of witchcraft. She countered by accusing him of slandering her good name. The local government officials—who included a cousin of her son William—threw him in jail. Undeterred, as soon as he was out, Ledrede had Alice arrested, along with her son and several of her servants.

Alice's friends helped her and one servant girl escape from the prison. But her servant Petronilla and her son William Outlaw had to face the church court on charges of heresy (turning their backs on the Catholic Church) and witchcraft.

Accused medieval witches were often tortured to force them to confess. Image courtesy of Wikimedia.

William Outlaw confessed to heresy. He was ordered to give a great deal of money to the poor and the church. Petronilla confessed to witchcraft—after being tortured by Bishop Ledrede's inquisitors. She said that she had met a demon and learned from him how to make potions. When the inquisitors searched Alice's house, they found ointments that they claimed were magical.

It's possible that Petronilla and Alice had been practicing some form of folk magic. Petronilla might even have believed she saw a demon. But people will say a lot of things when they're being whipped, burned, or deprived of food or sleep and they want the torture to stop.

Petronilla's confession under torture did not save her. Confession didn't save the accused witches in later witch trials, either. The accused usually had two choices: confess and die as a repentant witch or don't confess, be tortured longer, and die as an unrepentant witch. They were usually poor and powerless. By the time they were accused, they had already lost.

Petronilla was burned at the stake as a heretic and a witch. Her fate would be shared by perhaps 50,000 other women and men in the next two centuries.

Thousands of women and men were killed during the European witch hunts. Image courtesy of Wikimedia.

So, what really happened in this strange and sad case?

Alice outlived four husbands. Europeans in the Middle Ages often married more than once in their lives. Between diseases, wars, and accidents, people's spouses might die young and leave them alone or with young children. It was less lonely and easier to survive with a husband or wife, so remarriage was common. Alice's husbands could have died of natural causes. Men were often older than their wives and did more dangerous work. But Alice certainly had more husbands than most Medieval women, and she benefitted from their deaths by inheriting money or property from each one of them.

What about her last husband's accusation that she was poisoning him? It's possible. Maybe she realized that her husbands' early deaths benefitted her. Maybe she didn't like the control that marriage gave her husband over her money. She could have slipped poison into his food. But given how many deadly things were already in people's food and drink with the lack of refrigeration and clean water, it's also possible that he was already ill and suspicious of his wife because of her previous marriages. Without modern science to examine his body for toxins, we can't know if she poisoned him or not.

As for the magical ointments, we have no way now of knowing what they contained. One was said to make Alice's broom fly—quite an invention if it worked! Petronilla confessed that they made the potions with ingredients like dead men's fingernails, roosters sacrificed to the devil, and the hair of unbaptized boys. She might have been saying what she thought the inquisitors wanted to hear. Since women tended to run the kitchen as well as brewing drinks and making medicines in Medieval Europe, the men might have seen something sinister in common household ointments. Yet it was also possible for women to use their knowledge to brew up potions they believed were magic—or poisons.

*Medieval women's work in the kitchen meant they had
opportunities to poison people—on purpose or on accident.
Image courtesy of Wikimedia.*

Alice also might have poisoned one or more of her husbands by accident. If you've ever cooked and accidentally added too much milk or confused the salt for the sugar, you know how easy it is to make a mistake in the kitchen. Now, imagine that you were cooking with ingredients that could kill. Many medieval medicines were based on plants that are mildly or even extremely toxic, especially if someone took too much. Women were expected to know safe recipes, but a small mix-up could be deadly for their patients and themselves.

Then, were Alice Kyteler or Petronilla witches? Maybe. It's very difficult to tell if Medieval people accused of witchcraft considered themselves witches. Some of the thousands of people executed for witchcraft might have been trying to gain power or wealth or get revenge on their enemies through spells. Others may have been following traditional practices that they didn't even realize weren't really part of their religion. An example could be saying a chant for good luck while making bread. It would seem innocent unless an inquisitor thought it sounded unchristian. Most of the accused were probably uneducated, confused, and frightened to be brought before the inquisitors. Some probably suffered from mental illnesses that made them say or do strange things.

Also, witchcraft could be difficult to define. There was often a fine line between normal women's activities and what was seen as witchcraft. Making medicine was acceptable for a woman, and so was praying, but if a woman prayed to saints to help one of her medicines, that could look like she was invoking magic instead of just making a medicine. Though some men were executed for witchcraft, women made up about 75 percent of the victims of witch hunts. Part of this was because women engaged in regular household activities that men and sometimes other women might find suspicious.

So, Alice might have been guilty of poisoning her husbands. She might have even been practicing witchcraft. She was definitely guilty of deserting her servant Petronilla to a terrible death. Alice vanished after escaping from jail, never to be seen again. Rumor said she fled to England or Flanders. She probably changed her name, and there's no record of her after her escape. If she was a black widow, maybe she found new victims overseas.

8
PALACE IN THE CLOUDS

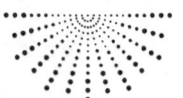

High in the Andes mountains of South America, Incan buildings perch thousands of feet above the river below. The buildings sit on a major fault line, prone to serious earthquakes, but their stone walls are intact after hundreds of years. The buildings have carved stones for tracing the movement of the sun, a sacred cave, and stairs that lead to nowhere. The enormous stones would have taken hundreds of people to move—the work of a lifetime—but the buildings were abandoned with no sign of a struggle. Why did the Incas build in such a remote location, and why did they desert their work?

The Incas rose to power in the 1200s. They united many peoples along the Pacific Coast of South America into an empire of 10 million people. That's twice as large as the mighty Aztec Empire of Mexico. They had the largest empire in the Americas before the arrival of Europeans.

The word Inca referred to the leaders of the people, but

today the term also describes the common people and their culture. They never invented the wheel or steel tools, but they built roads that were perfectly smooth over rough mountain terrain to connect their far-flung empire. They didn't use writing but kept records using a system of knots and strings that no one can read today. The Incas could even perform brain surgeries with an 80 to 90 percent success rate. But their most impressive achievements were their architecture.

Machu Picchu is located in the Andes Mountains in what is now Peru.

The Incas didn't pay taxes with money. Instead, the people had to donate their time and their work to building and maintaining the roads and palaces of the empire. It took tremendous work to cut stones, move them into place, and then lift them to create huge buildings. The stones fit together so perfectly that you can't slip a piece of paper between them, yet nothing holds them in place except gravity. Despite the numerous earthquakes and volcanos in the Andean region, many Incan walls are still standing after hundreds of years.

Incan stonework has survived hundreds of years of earthquakes. Photo courtesy of pxhidalgo via Deposit Photos.

Modern engineers and architects don't know how the Incas crafted such perfect buildings. The Incas used stones that were already in the area where they wanted to build. Historians think that they used wood spikes and water to crack the stones. The blocks sometimes weighed as much as 100 tons and had to be lifted into place. We still don't know how they moved such heavy stones, especially in remote, mountainous places like Machu Picchu.

The Incas worshipped the sun. Their most important building was the temple to the sun god in their capital at Cusco. The temple was called Coricancha or Golden Temple. It was built of stone and the walls were covered in gold. The temple was large enough to hold 4,000 people. It also housed the mummies of former emperors.

When the Spanish conquered the Incas, they stripped off the gold to send back to Spain. Then they tore down part of the temple and built a church in its place. An earthquake later destroyed the Spanish parts of the building, but the remaining Incan walls are still standing. The Spanish rebuilt their church around them.

The Incan walls of Coricancha still support this more recent church. Image courtesy of RobertCHG via Deposit Photos.

In comparison to Coricancha, Machu Picchu is small. It housed fewer than a thousand people. Archeologists have found no gold there. The Spanish couldn't have stolen Machu Picchu's treasures because they never found its remote location. Either it didn't have any gold or the Incas took it all away when they left.

The locals who lived near Machu Picchu later knew it was there, but they weren't interested in living in such a remote place either. The view is stunning, but it's not a welcoming place. It's difficult to reach and high in the mountains, easily overtaken by the cloud forests of the Peruvian mountains. Anyone who lived there would have to constantly chop back the trees.

It wasn't a natural place to build, either. The Incas had to start their construction by filling in the space between the two mountain slopes and adding stonework underground to support the buildings.

The Incas built Machu Picchu in a high and difficult location. Photo courtesy of mbisof via Deposit Photos.

So, what was the purpose of Machu Picchu? Why go to so much trouble to build in such a high and distant place? That is the greatest mystery of the palace in the clouds.

Machu Picchu was big enough to support perhaps 500 to 700 people. Out of an empire of 10 million people, that's not a large number—smaller than most modern towns. But people did live there—or at least died there. About 200 burials have been discovered at Machu Picchu, the skeletons of men and women. They appear to have died peacefully and not as sacrifices.

People buried at Machu Picchu came from different parts of the Incan Empire. Several of the skulls have a strange, almost alien appearance. They're much longer than typical human skulls. This has led some people to suggest that Machu Picchu was an outpost for extraterrestrials. A somewhat less exciting explanation is that some upper-class people from the Incan Empire bound their skulls with tight cords from a young age to make their heads grow longer.

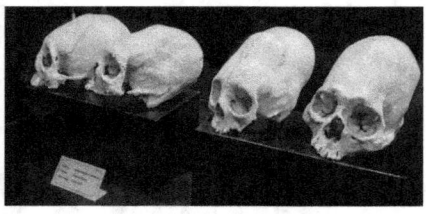

Incan skulls probably made unusually long by binding the skulls from childhood. Photo courtesy of videobuzzing via Deposit Photos.

Two-hundred burials are a large percentage of the number of people who lived at Machu Picchu. Some people suggest that Machu Picchu could have been a prison— difficult to reach or escape from, and a final stop for the royal family's enemies. On the other hand, it could have been a retirement village for elderly nobles or priests and priestesses. Or maybe the burials are there for some other reason that we haven't discovered yet.

Machu Picchu has several sacred buildings, including a temple to the sun and another to the moon. It also has several carved stones used for marking the passing of the sun, moon, and stars—all sacred to the Incas. Machu Picchu could have been a monastery or convent for religious men and women to study the heavens. Holy women were especially important in Incan religion. They performed many tasks for the emperor and helped with his religious duties.

This may have been a place for them to live and work apart from the distractions of everyday life. The site would have been dark and close to the heavens they hoped to study and understand.

Machu Picchu is also surrounded by terraces that were designed to capture and funnel water. This was not only important for controlling the runoff from storms, but it would also allow the Incas to grow crops at Machu Picchu. They couldn't grow enough crops to support everyone who lived there, though. The complex water system and terraces lead some scholars to think it might have been a place for agricultural experiments. Trying to keep 10 million people fed would be a difficult task for the Incan emperors, especially in steep mountain areas. So, they may have been studying ways to make it easier to grow crops in difficult terrains. The site could even have been a double scientific outpost for studying both crops and the stars.

The terraced slopes used to collect water and grow food.
Photo courtesy of PabloDamonte via Deposit Photos.

Some historians believe Machu Picchu was a summer palace for the royal family. It could have been a place for them to gather away from the sprawling city. The Incan emperor was supposed to be a descendant of the sun god, so it would be fitting for him to have a palace high above everyone else. But the royal family had several other, grander homes, so why would they need Machu Picchu as well? It might have made a good military retreat for the royal family, but this was not where they went to make their final stand against the Spanish. That happened at Ollantaytambo and then the hidden fortress of Vilcabamba. Both of those could hold more people than Machu Picchu. As the Incas fought elsewhere, Machu Picchu was forgotten.

Some people have wondered why some of Machu Picchu's walls started with large stones and ended with small ones. Was there a shortage of stones or labor that made it difficult to complete? Photo courtesy of byelikova via Deposit Photos.

Another possible use for Machu Picchu was as a pilgrimage site—a holy place that people walked to as part of a sacred journey to worship and learn. That would explain the various small temples and sacred symbols of Machu Picchu. It could also explain the mummies kept there, as Incas would consult the dead for wisdom. And the other burials could have been of priests and priestesses who took care of the site. Regardless of whether Incan pilgrims visited the site, Machu Picchu is a popular site for visitors today, with over a million people traveling to Peru each year to see the palace in the clouds—far more than probably saw Machu Picchu in the time of the Incas.

There are still many parts of Machu Picchu that are covered with jungle or have not yet been excavated. There's at least one chamber in Machu Picchu that has never been opened. Some scientists who used radar to see inside think it might contain gold and silver—and answers about Machu Picchu's mysteries. Officials worry that opening the chamber could endanger the structure. They are not convinced that there's anything inside worth the risk. But eventually, maybe a new discovery at Machu Picchu will reveal the secrets of the palace in the clouds.

Llamas were important to the Incas for their wool and for carrying supplies in the treacherous mountains, but they are not strong enough to have carried the stones for Machu Picchu. Image courtesy of sunsinger via Deposit Photos.

9

THE PRINCES IN THE TOWER

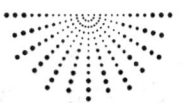

In 2012, historians and archeologists went on a quest for a lost king. Richard III had been killed in battle in 1485 by Henry Tudor, ending the War of the Roses over the English throne. Henry Tudor was the founder of the royal dynasty that included Henry VIII, famous for beheading his queens, and his daughter Elizabeth I, who refused to marry and ruled her kingdom alone. Richard III was remembered as a hunchback and a villain who cheated, lied, and murdered his way to the throne before Henry Tudor rid the world of him and dumped him in a forgotten grave.

But history is written by the winners, and recent historians have questioned the stories handed down by the Tudors. To learn more about who Richard III was, they wanted to find his lost grave.

They searched for the ruins of churches near the site of that last battle. They discovered where an ancient church had once stood, but the location was under modern buildings and parking lots. What were the chances that, after 500 years, the forgotten grave of a much-hated king could still be discovered? With only a thread of hope, they decided to dig under the parking lot.

And they found graves.

The archeologists were in luck. Though, as they examined the burials, they realized that grave robbers had plundered some of the burials. The odds that they would find Richard III shrunk further.

Richard III. Is this the face of a killer? Or a leader burdened by pain or worry? People see many different things in Richard's portrait. Image courtesy of Wikimedia.

Then, they discovered a strange grave. It was shallow—barely beneath the level where the church's stone floor once lay—and had been dug too short, so the body had been shoved in at an awkward angle without a coffin. As if the person was buried in a hurry. Even more exciting, the bones showed the person had likely died of battle wounds, and that he had a curved back. Like a hunchbacked king.

DNA tests confirmed that they had found Richard III. His strange grave had gone unnoticed by grave robbers, and also by the later Victorian residents of the site, who had built an outhouse right above the king's feet, which might explain why his feet bones were missing. Regardless, after 500 years, King Richard III was lost no more.

On studying the bones, scientists found that King Richard was not a hunchback, but he did have scoliosis, a curve in his spine that would have made one shoulder higher than the other. The hunchback story was exaggerated by his enemies after his death.

Which other stories about Richard had been exaggerated? The most notorious and wicked of the rumors about Richard III was that he secured the throne by murdering his two young nephews—the Princes in the Tower—who vanished without a trace during his short reign. How much of that story was true?

The Princes in the Tower were the twelve-year-old King Edward V and his nine-year-old brother Richard, the Duke of York. Their father, King Edward IV died in 1483, leaving the boys in the care of his brother, their uncle—the future Richard III. England was in the midst of the War of the Roses over who should hold the throne, so having a boy king with no experience fighting or ruling was not ideal. Richard brought the princes to the Tower of London, which served as a royal residence as well as a prison.

The mystery of the Princes in the Tower has intrigued people for centuries. This painting from the 1800s imagines the two young brothers in the Tower. Image courtesy of Wikimedia.

Perhaps because of fears of having a young, inexperienced king during a time of war, or perhaps at his uncle Richard's prodding, grumblings spread about young Edward V's right to be king. His mother, Elizabeth Woodville, came from a family of wealthy commoners rather than nobles. And Edward IV had married Elizabeth in secret because his advisors wanted him to marry a French princess instead to strengthen his hold on the throne. Some said that Edward IV had promised to marry someone else before he married Elizabeth—and in those days, promises of marriage were legal contracts. Now, people questioned whether the dead king's marriage was legitimate, and if the boys should have any claim to the throne. And if Edward V wasn't king, then who was?

It didn't take Richard III long to declare himself ruler instead of young Edward V. Many of the nobles supported him, though some threatened to remove Richard III and install Edward V as king instead.

And then, Edward and his brother disappeared.

They had been seen from time to time playing on the grounds of the Tower of London. A doctor had been brought in to attend to Edward V. Then, they were seen less and less, until they finally vanished as if they had never been in the Tower.

The Tower of London was both a royal palace and a prison. Were the princes guests or prisoners here? Image courtesy of Charlie Marshall CC BY 2.0.

Richard III met his fate on the battlefield in 1485, and no one ever discovered what happened to the Princes in the Tower.

Not long after the boys disappeared—while Richard III was still alive—rumors spread that he had murdered them so they could not steal his throne. This idea was encouraged by Henry VII when he defeated Richard and took the throne. Later, William Shakespeare, who worked for Henry VII's granddaughter, Queen Elizabeth I, wrote the play Richard III portraying the defeated king as a physical and moral monster, hunchbacked and murderous. That is the image of him that stuck for many years. When two skeletons were found beneath a staircase in the Tower of London in 1678, everyone assumed it was the two lost princes, and the bones were moved in with the royal burials in London's Westminster Abbey.

The white box in the back of this picture contains the bones found in the Tower and moved to Westminster Abbey—but who do the bones belong to? Image courtesy of amanderson CC BY 2.0.

But, in modern legal terms, all of this is circumstantial evidence. Richard was away from London when the boys disappeared, giving him an alibi, but he could have ordered his servants to kill the princes. Some of them might have been loyal enough to do it, and rumors claimed that they had, but there's no proof it ever happened.

If we want to try to solve this missing persons mystery from hundreds of years ago, we must examine the various theories about what happened to the boys and decide which one we think is most likely.

Maybe Richard III had the princes killed. He had a motive: keeping the throne. Some nobles led rebellions against Richard, wanting to make Edward V king, and it was at about that time that the princes vanished. Richard had generally been considered a good man, loyal to his brother and to England. That was why many people had wanted him to be king. But power corrupts, as the saying goes, and maybe Richard decided he didn't want to give up the throne and that it would be easier if the boys just disappeared. It would be a terrible thing to kill two children you were sworn to protect, but Richard might have even convinced himself it was necessary to stop the fighting and keep England safe. Without a confession from him or his servants, it would be hard to prove.

But as much as silence can hide the truth, it can also be revealing. None of the boys' family members ever accused Richard III of their deaths, including their mother, Elizabeth Woodville. During his lifetime, they might have been afraid to speak up, but once he was gone, it could have helped them gain favor with Henry Tudor if they denounced Richard III—even if they only suspected him of murder. But none of them ever did.

Elizabeth Woodville. What secrets did she know about the fate of her two missing sons? Image courtesy of Wikimedia.

Perhaps, then, Richard III didn't hurt his nephews. If the boys weren't murdered by their uncle, though, what happened to them?

One potential explanation is that Richard didn't kill the boys but one of his supporters did without his permission. Since the princes were under Richard's protection, he might have been afraid people wouldn't believe his innocence, so he covered up the murders. Richard had a falling out with his friend, the Duke of Buckingham, around the time that the princes went missing. Did Buckingham eliminate the princes to help Richard—or even himself, since he was also a contender for the throne?

Some people have also suggested that the princes' doctor, John Argentine, might have poisoned them. He had the opportunity and the ability to do so, but no clear motivation, so it's only a possibility.

Speaking of the doctor, another theory is that the boys died of an illness and Richard III hid the truth, again because he knew how bad it would look for him. Edward V had been reported to be in low spirits. This isn't surprising for a twelve-year-old prince who was separated from his family and advisors and told he was no longer going to be king. He might have been depressed. But he also could have been ill. The doctor could have been visiting just to check on the boys, but he might have been treating some deadly disease that finally claimed them.

Other people point a finger at Richard III's conqueror, Henry Tudor, who became King Henry VII as the murderer of the princes. What if, after defeating Richard III, dumping his body under the future outhouse-turned-parking lot, and returning in triumph to London, he was horrified to discover that young King Edward V, a rival for the throne, was living in hiding in the Tower of London or another royal residence? It might have been easy enough for him to dispose of the two boys and continue on his merry way to the throne.

A twist in this theory is that Henry Tudor married the boys' older sister, Elizabeth of York, to unite the divided realm. For this to work, he had to undo Richard III's declaration that Elizabeth Woodville's children were not legitimate heirs to the throne. But if Elizabeth of York was legitimate again, so were the Princes in the Tower—and if they were alive, they were the rightful rulers. A predicament for a would-be king.

*King Henry VII holding roses as a reminder that he ended
the War of the Roses by killing Richard III and claiming the
throne. Image courtesy of Wikimedia.*

Henry Tudor might have killed the boys and married their sister, all to secure his claim on the throne, but would Elizabeth have gone along with it? Women in the Middle Ages had far fewer choices then than they do today, but they weren't entirely powerless, and they could usually refuse a marriage. Of course, Elizabeth could have been pressured into it, or she could have been unaware of what happened to her brothers. But there's no proof that Henry VII killed the boys either.

What if the princes didn't die in the Tower? A supporter might have helped them escape. Richard III also might have hidden his nephews away to protect them from being kidnapped by other people who wanted to control the throne. When people accused him of harming the boys, he might have kept their location secret to keep them safe, even while malicious rumors swirled around him. If that is the case, and he did it to protect his nephews and England, then he was heroic for allowing people to say terrible things about him to protect his family and his country. Or, when the rumors spread, he might have already sent them out of the country for their safety and his, making it impossible for him to prove they were alive.

Several men came forward years later claiming to be the younger prince, Richard Duke of York. Percy Warbeck is the most famous of these "pretenders." He bore a strong resemblance to Edward IV and claimed that Edward V had been killed but he, Richard IV, had been sent overseas and was now old enough to return and claim his throne. Many people rallied around him, including the princes' aunt, the Duchess of Burgundy. He was captured by Henry VII's forces and confessed under torture to be an imposter—not the most reliable way to get the truth. Henry VII kept him alive for a while but eventually executed him. Many people believe he was related to Edward IV even if he wasn't Richard because the family resemblance was so strong.

King Edward IV and Percy Warbeck

Why did no one ever claim to be Edward V? Maybe because he could be proven to be dead, or maybe because he was still alive elsewhere. Philippa Langley, the same historian who helped discover Richard III's missing grave, points to a grave in a remote Devon church that's decorated with a stained-glass window of Edward V for no apparent reason. The grave belongs to a John Evans who appeared suddenly in the town in 1484—the same year the princes vanished—was immediately made a Lord of the Manor, and lived out his life in the remote village. Perhaps a king in exile?

When discussing the theories about the fates of the Prince in the Tower, we can't ignore the bones. All of them. Because there are two sets of extra bones in royal tombs that we have to account for.

The first are the bones found in the Tower. They were found when a staircase leading out of the tower was removed in 1674. The stairs had been built after the time of Richard III, and these were not the first bones found buried in the Tower. The workers initially found the bones, thought, "Eh, another day, another dead body hidden in the Tower," and tossed the bones into the pile of rubble. Not the best way to treat a potential crime scene.

Only later did someone make the connection between the bones and the story of the missing princes. Even though the staircase had been built after Richard III's time, it was possible that the bones belonged to the princes and had been hidden there, and thanks to Shakespeare, everyone knew the story of the villainous uncle who murdered his nephews for the throne. In 1678, the bones were laid in Westminster Abbey with the remains of other kings and queens. It wasn't until 1933 that doctors and scientists convinced the Dean of Westminster to let them have a look at the bones. Among other things, considering that pets, livestock, and even wild animals had been kept at the Tower over the centuries, they wanted to be sure the bones were even human.

It turns out they were, mostly—no one's pet monkey had been buried with the kings and queens of England in Westminster Abbey, but there were some chicken bones mixed in with the others. Royal chickens, we must assume.

But science in 1933 was not nearly as advanced as it is today. They couldn't examine DNA, for one thing. They measured the bones and teeth and took x-rays and determined that the bones could have been those of two boys about the ages of the princes. Essentially, they couldn't prove that the bones did not belong to the princes. Good enough, the bones were sealed back up again.

The measurements and X-rays have been pored over ever since. Some people have concluded that the bodies were too young or too old. Some have suggested that they were girls and not boys. We don't know for sure that they are related without being able to do DNA studies, which are difficult on remains that old and badly disturbed—and besides, Westminster Abbey refuses to allow further testing. A petition to require further DNA testing—one that would have been binding upon the British Parliament to consider—was shut down before it had the opportunity to gather the signatures required. Interesting, that, as if someone doesn't want to find the answers—or maybe admit a mistake.

But one thing stands out in the x-rays of the skulls: the

older or bigger of the two had serious jaw problems. Medieval European dental care and hygiene were pretty primitive, and even princes wouldn't have made it to old age with most of their teeth, but this person's jaw was literally crumbling away from the inside, perhaps due to a rare disorder known as histiocytosis X, which usually affects young males. We don't have any evidence that Edward V had this painful condition. Doctors have concluded that the disease by itself would not have killed him—or whoever the jaw belonged to—but it would have made life less pleasant without modern medical care. It might have contributed to other health problems, which could have killed the owner of the skull. But until Westminster allows DNA testing and other studies on the bones, we won't know for certain if they belonged to the princes or what killed them.

But those aren't the only bones for us to wonder about.

In 1789, workers were making repairs on St. George's Chapel of Windsor Castle, another resting place for many royals. They accidentally broke through into a forgotten vault that contained the bodies of Edward IV and Elizabeth Woodville. Next to these two coffins were two smaller coffins that were labeled as George and Mary, two of Edward IV's children who died young. The workmen sealed the vault back up and put up a plaque marking the burials. But then in 1810, two more coffins were found, one of them clearly marked as Edward IV's son George. These coffins were moved to the vault with Edward IV, but no one stopped to wonder about George and Mary's other coffins. The vault has remained sealed to this day, along with its two coffins for George and two coffins for Mary—or, perhaps the coffins of

George, Mary, Edward V and Prince Richard, the two princes secretly reunited with their parents after death?

Previous monarchs have refused to allow the vault to be disturbed again, but if that changes, we might answer at least one of the mysteries of the Princes in the Tower. Modern genetics researchers have identified living relatives of the princes, which would allow a DNA match to be made with the correct set of remains. And if we knew where the princes were buried, we might also know how they died. That might not answer the question of who did it, but perhaps it would—as historians learned in the case of Richard III's graves, bones hold many secrets.

10

THE STOLEN CITY OF ZIMBABWE

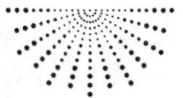

How could someone steal an entire city? It might seem impossible, but people have torn down or moved ancient buildings and monuments by taking the stones one by one. The stones of Great Zimbabwe in southern Africa are still mostly intact. People stole something more important from the Medieval city: its memory and identity. Great Zimbabwe impressed later explorers so much that they wanted to give their own people the credit for building it. They also wanted to take credit away from the Shona people of southern Africa whose ancestors created the city. Even now, there's much we don't know about Great Zimbabwe because of the stolen stories and artifacts. Enough is left, though, to show that it was one of the wealthiest and most impressive cities of the Middle Ages.

The word Zimbabwe means "stone houses." The Shona historically raised cattle and goats. They also farmed beans and sorghum. They crafted sculptures and used music to communicate with their ancestors. Perhaps most importantly for their history, they mined and worked precious metals, including copper and gold. Huge amounts of gold.

The region around Great Zimbabwe was rich with gold mines. Image courtesy of joreasonable via Deposit Photos.

The site of Great Zimbabwe is surrounded by thousands of gold mines. That's probably why Great Zimbabwe was built. Settlement on the hill overlooking the site began before 900 AD. But the heart of Great Zimbabwe is a huge, circular structure called the Great Enclosure. It was probably built around 1100. The walls are twenty feet (six meters) wide and thirty-six feet (eleven meters) high. They are the second largest structure on the African continent—only the Great Pyramids of Egypt are larger. The largest building of Great Zimbabwe is made up of almost a million carefully cut stone blocks. They were laid on top of each other very precisely so the whole building is still standing hundreds of years later, even though no mortar was used to "glue" the pieces in place.

The tower in the Great Enclosure. Its purpose is a mystery. Image courtesy of joreasonable via Deposit Photos.

In this complex is a giant, round tower. The tower is thirty feet tall, or about three stories high, and eighteen feet wide. It wasn't a house, and we don't know what the people used it for. Perhaps it was symbolic—a religious structure, for instance. Guards could have used it to keep watch, or it might have been part of a royal ceremony. Smaller circular structures decorate the outside of the walls but don't have any clear function either. The purpose of the Great Enclosure surrounding the tower is also a mystery. Some people think it was part of a royal palace. Others think it was used as a storehouse for the community.

Outside of Great Zimbabwe are the ruins of many houses built of local mud brick. The city grew over time, and people built these houses to live close to it. About 20,000 people lived at Great Zimbabwe in the 1300s and 1400s. That's not big compared to modern cities, but for the time, it was a large city—as big as London. And there are ruins of other villages near Great Zimbabwe. They might have been independent, or they could have been ruled by the leaders at Great Zimbabwe. Maybe they were even enemies. One nearby city, Mapungubwe, was abandoned about the same time that Zimbabwe reached its greatest size. Did Zimbabwe drive the people away from Mapungubwe, or were the people moving from one city to the other? Or something else entirely? We simply don't know.

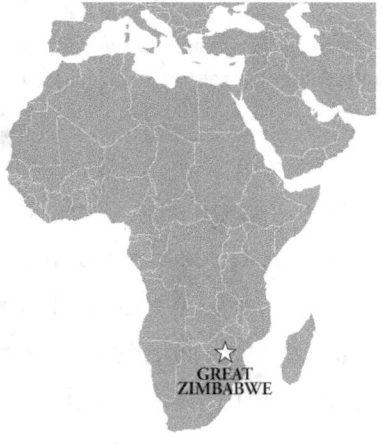

Great Zimbabwe's location between so many mines made it an important center for trade.

While we don't know much about Great Zimbabwe, we do know what drew all those people there: money. Thanks to all the gold mines in the region, wealth and trade flowed through Great Zimbabwe. Historians estimate that almost half of the gold in the Medieval world came from around

Great Zimbabwe. We don't know if Zimbabwe's leaders controlled the mines or simply benefitted from the travel and trade that came from the mining. Either way, at its height, it must have been one of the wealthiest cities in the world. Many of the people who lived there were probably merchants and goldsmiths making jewelry for trade, based on the smithing equipment and gold jewelry plundered from the ruins in the past.

Though many things have been stolen from Zimbabwe over the centuries, archeologists have found pottery from Asia and coins from Arabia in the ruins. This shows that the people of Zimbabwe traded with people from all over the world. Archeologists also found gold necklaces left behind by the looters as if there was so much treasure there that a simple gold necklace wasn't worth stealing.

A replica of the carved stone birds found around Great Zimbabwe. Image courtesy of J. Patrick Fischer CC BY 3.0.

Also common at Great Zimbabwe are carvings and statues of birds, often sitting on columns. This bird symbol has never been found elsewhere in African archeology; it exists only in Zimbabwe. And it doesn't seem to be a specific bird that can be identified, but more of an abstract symbol. Archeologists guess that these might have been a symbol of the royal family or of deceased ancestors, but they don't know for certain what the birds mean.

In the 1400s, Great Zimbabwe began to decline. We can only guess at the reasons. Maybe there wasn't enough food to support the population. Gold is lovely, but people can't eat it. Archeology shows some signs of drought, which would have made it harder to feed so many people. And it seems the amount of gold in the area declined as well, so people who were following the wealth may have moved to new, richer mining areas elsewhere. Maybe the government changed, or Zimbabwe lost some of its trading partners. It doesn't seem that there was a war there. It's more like the people slowly moved away until the site was eventually abandoned.

But the site wasn't entirely forgotten. The Shona people still visited there for religious ceremonies. This may hint at a religious purpose for the site during its height as well, one that the people did not forget.

Unfortunately, Great Zimbabwe was not to be left in peace. European rulers heard rumors by the 1500s of a great and incredibly rich city in Africa, and they wanted it. When the first European explorers reached the city, they were stunned. They couldn't imagine how the huge walls had been built. They didn't want to imagine that the African people living in huts nearby could have built such a huge structure—especially when the local people didn't remember who had built the structure. How would they when it had been there for hundreds of years?

The walls of Great Zimbabwe are still impressive today.
Image courtesy of PantherMediaSeller via Deposit Photos.

European colonists were hoping to steal the land and the rich mines from the local Shona. That was easier to justify if they could say that Great Zimbabwe was built by other people. Then, they were taking something that had been abandoned by other people and didn't belong to the locals. So, they made various guesses about Zimbabwe. It was a castle built by Europeans who had come there in the past. It was Solomon's Mines or the palace of the Queen of Sheba from the Bible. It had been a trading post of some Middle Eastern or Asian people. Anything to deny the Shona their heritage.

Then, European historians began to examine the site in the 1800s. Some said that the castle or Biblical theories were ridiculous. The items found around Great Zimbabwe were clearly similar to those used by later Shona people. The European leaders didn't want to listen to that. Other historians came along who were determined to prove that this site was European or Middle Eastern. They explored the ruins and destroyed anything that provided a connection to the people of Africa. One of these self-appointed archeologists dug down several feet around the tower in the Great Enclosure, throwing away nearly everything he found because it was of African origin.

Other so-called archeologists stole anything they considered valuable—including gold and some of the soapstone bird carvings. They trashed the rest of their findings, such as pottery and metal tools. And when these untrained "archeologists" did save an item, they didn't record exactly where they found it or what was found nearby. That is essential in archeology, where, ideally, an item is studied where it is found to discover as many clues as possible. What clues might they have uncovered and destroyed—information about the gold mining, the size of the city, the bird symbols, or even why the city declined? But those are all lost now.

Using the justification that the ruins and the mines didn't belong to the Shona, the European powers conquered Zimbabwe and the Shona people. They created a country they called Rhodesia after a British explorer. In the process, they destroyed clues about the history of Zimbabwe, leaving us with many mysteries about the city and its downfall.

But the Shona and their neighboring peoples didn't forget Great Zimbabwe entirely. They fought for many years against the English colonizers who controlled their country and its wealth. And they used Great Zimbabwe as proof that they could direct their own fortunes. In the 1960s and 1970s, the English-controlled government banned any books that discussed Great Zimbabwe or suggested it was built by native Africans. The truth was dangerous. In 1980, the African people of Rhodesia finally won their independence. They called their new country Zimbabwe after the ruins. They included the bird figure on their national flag, a reminder that part of their history had been stolen, but they hadn't been erased. Now, African scholars are working to rediscover their history and solve the mysteries of Zimbabwe.

The flag of Zimbabwe with its bird symbol. Image courtesy of Steve_Allen via Deposit Photos.

11

DEADLY MEDIEVAL FLASH MOBS

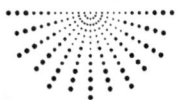

In 1518, in the European city of Strasbourg, a woman named Mrs. Troffea stepped into the street and started dancing. She wasn't celebrating. No, it seemed to observers that she wasn't happy to be dancing. But she kept going until she collapsed from exhaustion. When she recovered enough to get back on her feet, she began her dance again. Soon, other people joined her, dancing in the streets until their legs gave out. By the time this dancing rage ended weeks later, over one hundred people had danced themselves to death.

This was the last major outbreak of one of the strangest plagues in history: the dancing plague. It first appeared in Europe in the 1000s and occurred off and on until the 1500s. Like a scene from a musical or a medieval version of a flash mob, people in cities trickled into the streets to dance, and the trickle quickly became a flood. The dancers didn't stop to eat, drink, or sleep, sometimes begging for the dance to stop.

Priests and politicians tried to halt the outbreaks, but the dancing spread from city to city, with hundreds of people dancing in the streets day and night.

And then, as suddenly as it began, the dancing outbreak would stop. The survivors went about their lives completely cured, though probably footsore. Even today, we don't know exactly what caused these outbreaks of dancing mania in the Middle Ages.

No one knew how to help the people afflicted with the dancing plague. Image courtesy of Wikimedia.

Pandemics and plagues have been a problem for human settlements throughout history. The Middle Ages were no exception. Medieval Europe slowly recovered from the chaos of Rome's fall, and its countries developed stable governments. With less warfare, it was safe to travel farther from the protection of castles. This let people set up towns and cities where they traded food, goods, and ideas with those who lived farther away. Life in the "Dark Ages" looked a little brighter.

But they also traded germs.

The Middle Ages may be most famous for the Black Death that sprung up in the 1300s, sweeping through Asia, Europe, and North Africa. The Black Death killed millions of people. At least 1 out of every 3 people in Europe, Asia, the Middle East, and North Africa died of the disease. In some places, the death rate was almost 100 percent, with entire towns wiped out.

Though some Medieval cultures understood that good hygiene, like bathing and washing hands, was important for health, no one knew about germs until the 1800s when high-powered microscopes allowed people to see the tiny creatures causing so much misery. So, people in the Middle Ages lived with a variety of parasites and vermin. Fleas and bedbugs were very common—bloodsucking—companions. People sometimes drank and bathed in the same rivers where they washed their dirty clothes and where their animals pooped. This meant that almost everyone had intestinal worms at some point in their lives.

This doesn't mean that people liked living in dirty conditions. They generally tried to stay clean, but they didn't have things like flushing toilets and self-contained sewer systems to help them. When a plague such as the Black Death plowed through a city like cannonballs, entire families became sick and died. People didn't understand why it was happening. They didn't know that fleas carried by rats were spreading the disease. They thought it might be caused by bad smells or evil spirits.

When a Mongol army laying siege to a city came down with the Black Plague and the bodies piled up, the stink was nauseating. The surviving Mongol leaders decided to clean up by catapulting the rotting bodies into their enemies' city, thinking the bad smells would drive their enemies away. It did even more than that: it spread the Black Death through the city.

Trying to clean up bad smells usually helped to make things a little more sanitary, but not enough to get rid of the rats and fleas. Thus, the plagues continued to strike from time to time, throwing people into helplessness and panic. When plagues wiped out leaders, cities and even empires could collapse. When farm workers died, there was no one to plant and harvest grain and fruit or care for animals, bringing famine.

Facing the Black Plague, people fled from towns and cities, often spreading the disease farther and changing the whole pattern of where people lived and worked. On top of this, religious leaders seemed helpless to provide comfort and sometimes declared that the world was ending. In other words, lives in the late Middle Ages were full of stress, disease, and chaos.

In this setting, the dancing plague struck. The first instance is surrounded in legend, but it was supposed to have occurred in a town called Kolbigk in Saxony (now part of Germany) in about 1020. It was Christmas Eve, and the priest was holding services. Some of the villagers who were unhappy with the priest interrupted his service by starting a dance either inside the church or just outside of it. According to the legend, the priest then cursed the dancers so they could not stop dancing for an entire year.

The idea that the dancing plague was a curse lingered. In later outbreaks, priests sometimes said that the dancers were being punished by a vengeful saint or were possessed by evil spirits. The priests couldn't stop the dancing, though.

In other cases, some leaders thought the dancing was good for people—that those affected were dancing away poison, disease, or evil. Some cities even hired musicians to play for the dancers. No one knew what was causing the dancing plague, and they also didn't know how to stop it, so these people went along with it.

These victims of the dancing plague have musicians escorting them as they dance. Image courtesy of Wikimedia.

We don't know what caused the dancing plague either, but looking back through the lens of history, we can try to guess.

While the story of the plague's origin with an angry priest's curse is unlikely to be accurate, some people point to possible causes of the dancing plague found in the legend. The people in the original dancing plague story were dancing as a way to interrupt a priest they didn't like. Could people with the dancing plague have been dancing as a form of protest? They might have been pretending to be forced to dance so they wouldn't get in trouble for their disruptive behavior, but they were doing it to make leaders they didn't like look helpless or foolish. An argument against this explanation is that it would be an extreme form of protest when you consider that some of the dancers died.

Another possibility is the power of suggestion and mass hysteria. This is the theory that panicked reactions can be contagious. The Middle Ages were a time of great stress. Sometimes, people react to stress in odd ways, such as by fainting, laughing, shaking, or perhaps even dancing. And when we're told not to do something, like bite our fingernails or think of a pink elephant, that often becomes the thing we badly want to do. So, is it possible that people were dancing because they'd heard the legend of the dancing curse and were afraid that they might start dancing?

Their thinking might go, "I've heard there's another famine. I'm so worried about having enough to eat. What if the plague hits us again? What if we really are cursed?" Their eye twitches. "Oh, no. Does that mean I'm sick? What if my arms twitch, too? What if I start dancing like those other people did?"

Mass hysteria happens when one person's panic spreads to the people around them. Someone starts dancing, and before they know it, Medieval flash mob.

This can occur because our brains have mirror neurons. These are cells in our brains that react to what other people feel. They're the reason we get scared when characters are in danger in books or movies, wince when we see someone else get hurt, or laugh or cry along with our friends. They might have helped our ancestors survive by helping humans care for one another—and by making them react quickly in a dangerous situation where every moment could mean survival or death.

"If Ugg is scared and running from that thing with the teeth, I should be, too."

Mass hysteria occurs in modern times as well, with cases reported of groups of people shaking, fainting, laughing uncontrollably, or even developing symptoms of diseases with no obvious cause.

The dancing plague could be a case where a group of people facing a lot of stress and dangers saw one person dancing and their brains hijacked them into thinking that they should be dancing, too.

Of course, this theory assumes that someone must have started dancing in the first place and that it was something that people all across Europe were worried would happen to them. Sometimes, when strange events are labeled mass hysteria, it's because no one knows why it happened.

Another possible reason for the dancing plague is ergot poisoning. Ergot is a fungus that grows on grains, especially rye. Now we know about ergot and how to keep it out of our food, but people in the Middle Ages were not always so fortunate. If people ingest too much ergot, they get sick. Ergot poisoning can cause convulsions, which could look like attempts at dancing, as well as delusions and hallucinations. Medieval witch trials have been blamed on ergot poisoning causing people to see and hear strange things. Perhaps it could lead to groups of people dancing if they were all affected by ergot poisoning. But why would some people in the city get it and not others?

Ergot affecting a head of grain. Image courtesy of PantherMediaSeller via Deposit Photos.

Ultimately, we can't know what caused the dancing plague, or why the outbreaks stopped, but we're probably all glad that we only have to dance if we want to, and we can stop when our feet hurt.

12

YASUKE THE BLACK SAMURAI

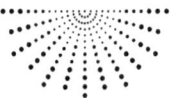

In 1582, a group of captured Japanese warriors were brought before the samurai general Akechi Mitsuhide. Mitsuhide looked over the men, prepared to kill them as captured enemies. But one of the men troubled him. This man was African, though he fought alongside the Japanese samurai. Mitsuhide wasn't sure what to do with this man. He wasn't Japanese and therefore didn't follow the same rules as the Japanese samurai.

"Banish him to the Christian church," Akechi decided.

The African samurai, Yasuke, was sent to the church. He was never heard from again. But just as mysterious as his fate is where he came from. How did an African man come to be fighting with the Japanese forces in a Japanese war for power?

Medieval Japan was ruled by an emperor, though true power often rested with the Japanese nobles. From the late

1100s on, these leaders were the shoguns, or military leaders from the samurai class. Similar to medieval Europe, the shoguns oversaw a feudal system of government. This was where the leading nobles gave their followers land in exchange for military service (either as knights or as samurai). The lower classes worked the land in exchange for protection or paid a portion of their earnings to their lord. The samurai lived in castles and used armor and the famous samurai swords. They practiced a strict code of loyalty, self-discipline, and bravery.

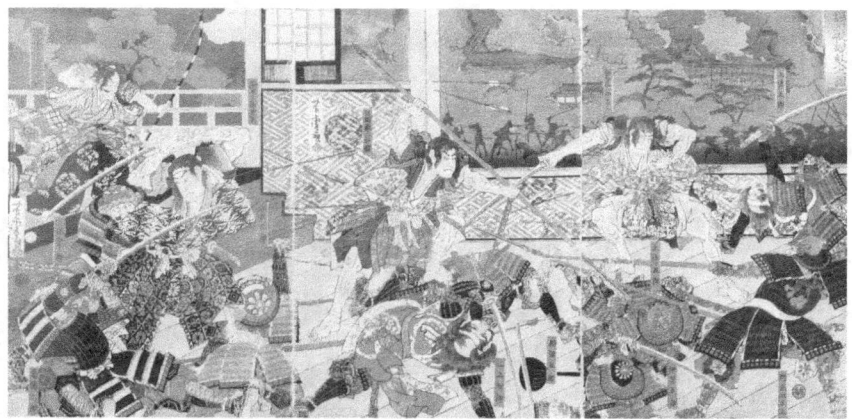

Samurai at war. Image courtesy of izzy74 via Deposit Photos.

But feudal systems of government have several problems (aside from the lack of freedom for almost all of the population). The noble with the largest army was usually the most powerful and wanted to be in charge. In Japan, the shoguns and their samurai sometimes fought for control of the country. In the 1400s and 1500s, this led to a period of civil wars in Japan. It was a deadly time, but also a time that a great fighter could rise to fame.

It was in this scene of constant warfare that Yasuke the Black Samurai made his mark.

We don't know where in Africa Yasuke came from. We also don't know his true name—Yasuke is a Japanese name. Reports say he spoke Swahili, so some historians guess he came from Mozambique in south-east Africa. Swahili wasn't the only language he spoke. He seemed to have a gift for picking up languages wherever he traveled, and he traveled from Africa, through India, and to Japan. We don't know why he traveled so far—if he couldn't return to his homeland or simply didn't wish to. He appeared to be free and not a slave, and to be traveling because he wanted to. He also seemed to thirst for adventure—after all, he was about to become the first non-Japanese samurai.

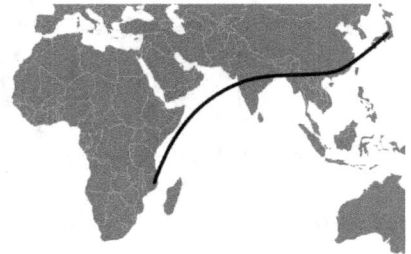

A possible route for Yasuke's travels if he traveled by sea and by land to Japan.

Yasuke arrived in Japan with some Jesuit missionaries from Portugal. By the 1500s, European nations had enough wealth and technological understanding to travel much farther in search of trade. Japan had been fairly isolated and would make an excellent trading partner with their advanced sword-making and ceramic skills. European leaders believed that by converting Japanese leaders to their version of Christianity, they would be the ones who would trade with Japan.

The Jesuits were Catholic. Yasuke may have become Catholic at some point in his travels, but he wasn't in Japan as a missionary. He was a bodyguard. The Jesuit priests were technically not allowed to travel with soldiers, so they hired "servants" who happened to be skilled fighters.

The Jesuits had some success converting Japanese leaders to Christianity, but none of the priests made the impression that Yasuke did. For one thing, Yasuke was over six feet tall—at a time when most Japanese men were closer to five feet. So, he towered over the Japanese people. Further, the Japanese leaders had never seen an African man before. They thought he dyed his skin with ink until he scrubbed it to show that he was really Black. People wondered if he was Buddha or another religious figure. They were so excited to see him, they crowded the streets where he went, sometimes crushing and stepping on each other to get a view of the tall man from Africa.

Oda Nobunaga was one of the unifiers of Japan. Image courtesy of Wikimedia.

Yasuke made an impression on the most powerful man in Japan: Oda Nobunaga. Nobunaga was the leading shogun in Japan at the time. Nobunaga was impressed by Yasuke's size, but even more so by his intellect. Yasuke learned Japanese quickly and told Nobunaga about his travels. He then introduced the arts-loving warlord to Utenzi—traditional Swahili poetry. Nobunaga was so impressed, he invited Yasuke to be one of the favored few who dined with him and discussed the important matters facing Japan.

Nobunaga also allowed Yasuke to train with his samurai. We don't know what kind of training Yasuke had received before, but he must have had some fighting skills to be a bodyguard. A Japanese painting from this time depicts a Black man sumo wrestling. Many historians believe it's Yasuke. He demonstrated the martial skills and discipline required to be a samurai. An outsider had never been invited to be a samurai before, but Nobunaga was so impressed that he made Yasuke one of his personal samurai. Yasuke left his work for the Jesuits to join Nobunaga's fight to unify Japan.

Many people think this image shows Yasuke training.
Image courtesy of Wikimedia.

For a while, Nobunaga looked like he was going to succeed in his quest. But then, one of his generals, Mitsuhide, betrayed him. Mitsuhide trapped Nobunaga in his house and set it on fire. Nobunaga only had 30 of his most loyal followers with him—including Yasuke. Knowing he could not win against this betrayal, and trapped in a burning house, Nobunaga ritually cut his stomach open. He then asked his closest attendant to cut off his head so that the traitor general could not claim victory over him. We don't know if Yasuke was the one who cut off his head, but it was Yasuke who took the shogun's head and escaped with it so Mitsuhide could not take Nobunaga's place as leader.

Claiming an enemy's head showed victory over him. Image courtesy of Wikimedia.

Yasuke joined Nabunaga's son as another civil war swept

over Japan. Unfortunately, Mitsuhide defeated Nabunaga's son as well. Yasuke was captured. All of the other samurai were executed, but Mitsuhide spared Yasuke and banished him to the Jesuits' church. We don't know why Mitsuhide didn't kill Yasuke. He would have known that Yasuke was one of Nobunaga's favorites. He might have respected Yasuke and not wanted to kill him. Or maybe he meant it as an insult, implying that Yasuke wasn't a real samurai.

Regardless of Mitsuhide's intent, Yasuke was the first of several great non-Japanese warriors who became samurai. And Mitsuhide was not a good enough general to unite Japan as Nobunaga had. Mitsuhide was defeated and killed as the civil war dragged on.

Yasuke disappeared from history after his capture by Mitsuhide. Maybe he did return to the Jesuits. It wasn't long after this that Christianity was banned in Japan for being too divisive, and many of the Christians were murdered. If Yasuke was Christian—or even if he was once again working as a bodyguard for them—he might have died alongside the people he had come to Japan to protect. But he seemed to have a restless need to wander, so maybe he moved on from Japan before that. He could have traveled back to India or Africa, or on to China, Europe, or the Americas. Wherever he went, he doubtless had many more adventures.

13

THE RACE TO THE "NEW WORLD"

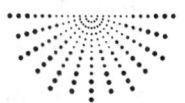

"In fourteen-hundred-and-ninety-two, Columbus sailed the ocean blue."

This old rhyme helps students remember the closing chapter of the Middle Ages. Christopher Columbus sailed from Spain to the Caribbean islands in 1492. He was looking for a faster route to Asia for trading spices and other valuable items. He didn't realize he had stumbled upon a different continent, so he called the native people "Indians." Columbus is admired by some for his bravery in trying a new route. He is hated by others for his terrible treatment of the native peoples. Regardless, his voyage connected two lands that had long been separated, changing the world forever.

Columbus's journey began a new era, but he was not the first European to reach the Americas. In fact, one of the mysteries of the Middle Ages is just how much contact the people of Africa, Europe, and Asia had with American peoples—and which of the "Old World" peoples reached the "New World" of the Americas first.

We know the Vikings of Scandinavia voyaged to the Americas around the year 1000. Their clever sailors had settlements on Iceland and Greenland. It wasn't much farther to reach what is now Canada. Norse sagas tell stories about a place the Vikings called Vinland and a people known to them as Skraelings. The Norseman Erik the Red established a settlement in Greenland when he was banished from Iceland for killing someone in a fight. His son, Leif Erikson (Erik's son), sailed farther west and established a colony on the land he found there.

The Norsemen or Vikings were some of the best sailors in the Medieval world. Image courtesy of algolonline via Deposit Photos.

Lief didn't stay in the colony, but his sister Freydis Eriksdottir (Erik's daughter) and his sister-in-law Gudrid both journeyed there. Gudrid gave birth to the first Norse baby—perhaps the first European baby—born in the Americas, a boy named Snorri.

Freydis's adventures also feature in some of the Norse sagas. They say when the Skraelings attacked her settlement, she was too pregnant to run. The Viking men escaped but left her behind.

"Cowards!" Freydis yelled at the men.

She grabbed a sword, ripped her shirt to reveal that she was a pregnant woman, and turned on the Skraelings to face them alone.

They took one look at her, said, "Nope, not today," and fled.

For a long time, no one was certain if these stories were really about the Vikings reaching the Americas, though people on the east coast of the United States sometimes claimed to discover Viking artifacts. But then, in the 1960s, archeologists searching for traces of the Vikings in North America discovered L'Anse Aux Meadows, the ruins of a settlement with Norse buildings and artifacts. This proved that the Vikings had been in America hundreds of years before Columbus.

Reconstruction of the Viking settlement in "Vinland" at L'Anse Aux Meadows, Canada. Photo courtesy of Dylan Kereluk CC BY 2.0.

We don't know how far the Vikings traveled in America.

Some people think they only landed on the coast of Canada, while others think they traveled south and west into the modern United States.

We also don't know why they left. Conflicts with the Native peoples may have driven them off, Freydis's efforts notwithstanding. Another possibility is that changes in the weather drove them away. They also settled Vinland before the Black Death began to spread in Europe. Once the plague hit Iceland in 1250, it wiped out much of the population. Perhaps there weren't more people to spare for the colony.

The disease smallpox also spread among the Vikings in waves, killing people each time. One of the mysteries of the Vikings in America is why smallpox or other European diseases didn't jump from them to the Native American populations.

After Columbus's contact, smallpox and other "Old World" diseases spread through the Native American nations. Native populations had never been exposed to these diseases. The Europeans, Africans, and Asians were alive because their ancestors had survived outbreaks of the Black Death, smallpox, measles, and the flu. They had developed some resistance to these germs. But Native American's bodies had never fought the new diseases. They had no immunity. "Old World" diseases killed up to 95% of the Native peoples.

The only reason this wouldn't have happened earlier was either that the Vikings who reached the Americas didn't carry the diseases or else they didn't have direct contact with the Native American populations.

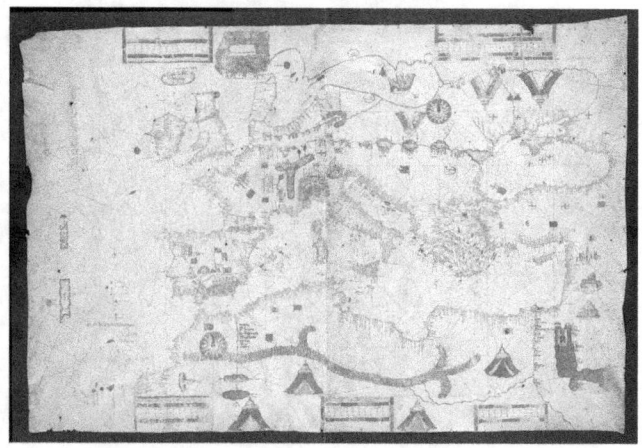

A European map from 1489 showing two rectangular islands in the west. Image courtesy of Wikimedia.

Many other European cultures have stories about people sailing west. Old European maps and myths often tell of a forgotten paradise to the West, such as Avalon or Antilia. The west is where the sun sets, so it could be that these paradises were symbolic of Heaven or an afterlife, but it could also be that early European sailors had discovered islands to the west.

For instance, the Celtic people have legends about early voyages to the Americas. One is about the Irish Saint Brendan the Navigator in the 500s and another is about the Welsh Prince Madoc in the 1100s. British explorer Tim Severin recreated the journey across the North Atlantic Ocean in an ancient Celtic vessel, proving that it would have been possible for Celts to reach the Americas. Some people think they have even found Ogham, the ancient Irish script, on engravings in the Americas, but historians haven't agreed on this.

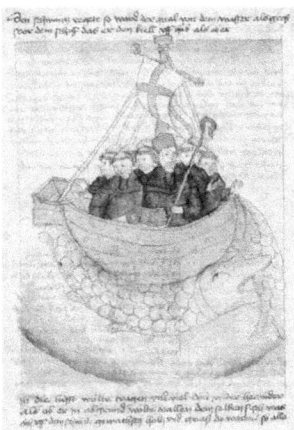

This Medieval image illustrates the story of Saint Brendan
the Navigator. Tim Severin proved it was possible to sail a
traditional Celtic boat like this one to North America.
Image courtesy of Wikimedia.

The Aztec god Quetzalcoatl is sometimes used as an argument that early Europeans reached the Americas. Quetzalcoatl is described as a white-skinned, bearded god who went into the East and promised to return. This could refer to a European visitor.

The Tecaxic-Calixtlahuaca head may be the best evidence for possible European contact with early American peoples. This carved head was found in the 1930s buried with Aztec artifacts from before the Spanish arrived. Yet it's not Aztec; it's Roman. Historians generally agree that it's real. It may show that Romans at some point reached the Americas and traded with peoples there. It's also possible that later explorers like Celts or Vikings brought the artifact. The head may have even arrived on a shipwreck washed ashore. Some people believe that the head was placed in the Aztec ruins as a modern hoax. It's not impossible. The people who discovered it are all dead, so we can't know for certain.

Does the presence of pyramids in Mexico and Egypt prove the two cultures had contact? Or did they each develop the style on their own? Image courtesy of sonar via Deposit Photos.

Africa also has several contenders for the first to reach the Americas. Early historians noted the similarities between American and Egyptian pyramids. They wondered if the two cultures had contact before Columbus. Two cultures could both have invented pyramids, but traces of the American tobacco plant have been found with Egyptian mummies. Possibly, the mummies were contaminated by modern archeologists who smoked tobacco in pipes, but there also could have been forgotten trade between the two cultures. Historians have proven that people could have sailed from Egypt to the Americas, but we don't know if they did.

The Mali Empire of West Africa may have sent explorers

to the Americas in the 1300s. Founded in the 1200s, Mali became a wealthy Arab-African Empire on the west coast of Africa. It stretched inward to Timbuktu, famous for its fabulous riches and learning. A Mali Mansa (ruler), called Mansa Musa, traveled across Egypt to Arabia. He told the people he met that the ruler before him, Mansa Muhammed ibn Qu, had sailed to a western land and never returned.

Timbuktu in the Mali Empire was a center of wealth and education—both helpful to explorers. Image courtesy of marzolino via Deposit Photos.

According to the story, Mansa Muhammad ibn Qu believed that it was possible to sail across the whole ocean, so he sent out a fleet of ships. He told them to keep sailing until they reached the end of the Atlantic or ran out of provisions. The ships reached a "great river" in the ocean—a strong current. One of the ships reported this to the emperor.

According to the story, the excited emperor set off in his ships to explore the ocean and never returned. Mansa Musa claimed that Mansa Muhammed left with 1,000 ships. This would probably be an exaggeration to show off the wealth of the Mali empire, since 1,000 ships and the men to steer them would have seriously depleted even such a wealthy empire.

But that doesn't mean a smaller expedition couldn't have reached the Americas. The great river in the ocean is likely the Canary Current. This strong current would easily carry ships from Africa to the Americas but would make it very difficult for any ships to sail back. This could explain why the ships went out but didn't return. The fact that the stories mentioned such a current at least shows that the West African sailors were familiar with the Atlantic Ocean.

Columbus supposedly heard rumors of ships sailing from West Africa to lands in the West. He also heard rumors in the Americas of dark-skinned people who had reached the Caribbean and had gold-tipped spears. Chemical analysis of the gold supposedly from these spears suggests it could have come from Africa, but there's no definite proof.

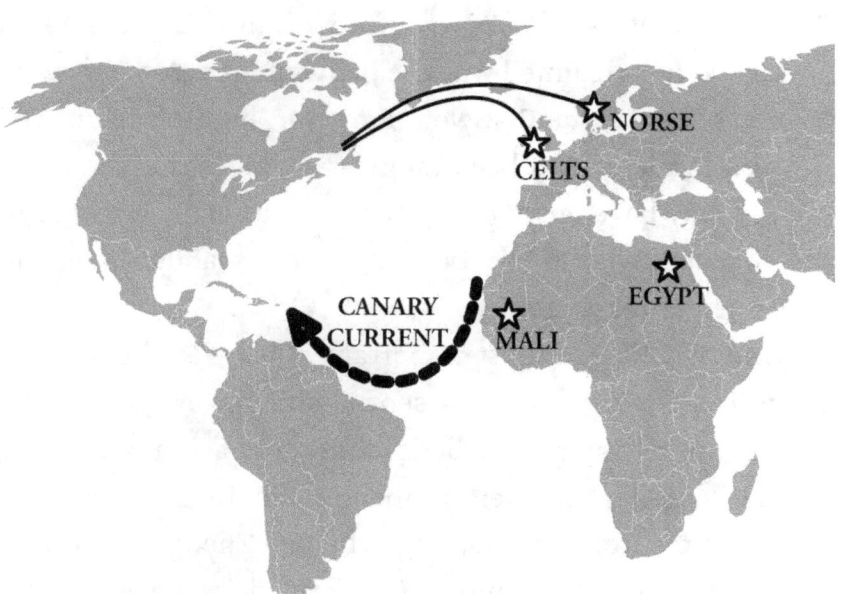

This map shows several possible routes across the Atlantic for explorers from Scandinavia, the Celtic nations of Ireland and Wales, and West Africa.

Asia and the Pacific Islands also have some strong contenders for winning the race to the Americas.

Genetic studies show a relationship between Polynesians and South American people. Considering how widely the Polynesians traveled, it would not be surprising that they had contact with the Americas. The Rapa Nui use of sweet potatoes—a food from the Americas—makes another strong argument for communication between the cultures. Though it is possible that sweet potatoes ended up in the ocean and floated to Pacific Islands, it's more likely that food was traded between South American and Pacific peoples.

The story of a lost Chinese emperor lies at the heart of a claim that Chinese explorers arrived in the Americas before Columbus. The Jianwen ("Civil") Emperor of Ming China, Zhu Yunwen, ruled China for a short time in the late 1300s. One of his uncles, Zhu Di, overthrew him and presented a burned body he claimed was the Jianwen Emperor. Yet many people believed the Jianwen Emperor had escaped. The Jianwen Emperor had been known as a kind and just ruler, so they may have only wished that he was alive. It's hard to know because his uncle burned histories about him and tried to erase his legacy.

One of Zhu Di's most important allies was the admiral Zheng He. The new emperor sent Zheng on several treasure expeditions. Many people believed he was actually hunting for the missing Jianwen Emperor. Whether or not the Jianwen Emperor escaped, and whether Zheng found him, Zheng was a great sailor. He traveled between China, Southeast Asia, India, Arabia, and Africa. Some historians think he also might have sailed as far as America. It's impossible to know for certain because later emperors destroyed the records of Zhu Di.

An illustration of the ships Zheng He used to explore much of the world. Courtesy of Wikimedia.

But even if Zheng didn't reach America in his impressive adventures, earlier Chinese explorers might have.

Chinese legends mention a mythical land to the east called Fusang. Some Chinese poems call Japan Fusang, but in the older stories about Fusang, it's a greater distance away—as far as the West Coast of North America. Fusang appears on a copy of a map brought back to Europe by explorer Marco Polo, who traveled from Italy to China in the 1200s. The copy appears to show Alaska, but we don't have the original map from the 1200s, so we don't know if it showed Alaska or if Alaska was added later.

It would not be difficult for explorers or traders to go from Asia to Alaska, though. In modern times, shipwrecked Japanese sailors have washed up on the west coast of the Americas, so it certainly could have happened in the past as well.

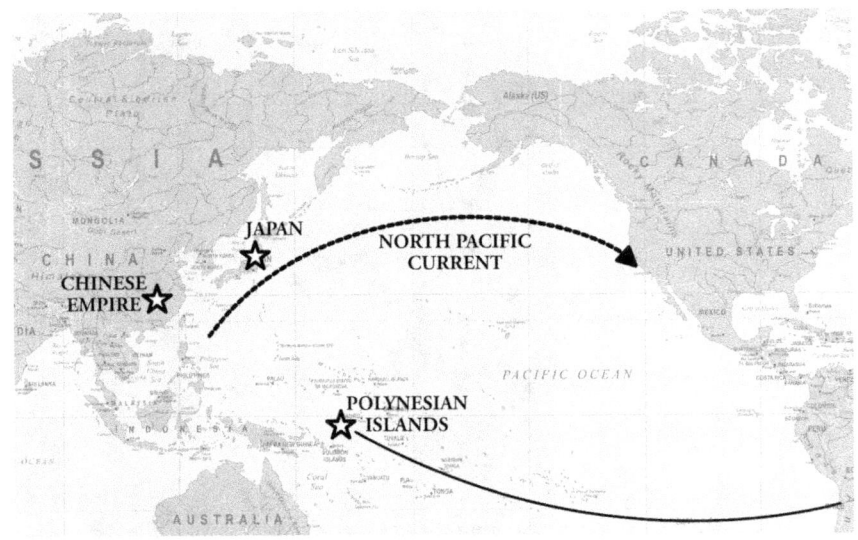

Russia and Alaska are so close that it would be fairly easy to travel from one to the other. Ocean currents—and the amazing navigational skills of Polynesian sailors—offer other routes from Asia to the Americas.

Though Columbus's voyage began the modern age by permanently connecting the two halves of the world, he was not the first non-Native person to reach the Americas. The Vikings settled on the coast of Canada. Africans, Asians, and other Europeans may have reached the Americas at various times as well. And did people from the Americas ever venture to the "Old World?" If so, their adventures are now buried among the mysteries of the past.

SELECTED SOURCES AND
FURTHER READING

Disclaimer: The author and publisher provide these links for informational purposes only and do not endorse or control the content of any resources listed below. Hyperlinks may become out of date and some sources may contain ads or information that is inaccurate, outdated, or sensitive. The author and publisher assume no responsibility or liability for the content of outside sources.

King Arthur

Andrew Breeze, "The Name of King Arthur," *Mediaevistik*, Vol. 28 (2015), pp. 23-35.

Gildas, "Concerning the Ruin of Britain," Fordham University Medieval Sourcebook, https://sourcebooks.fordham.edu/source/gildas.asp

Nennius, "The History of the Britons, 8th Century," Fordham University Medieval Sourcebook, https://sourcebooks.fordham.edu/source/nennius.asp

Greek Fire

Richard Groller, "Greek Fire: The Best Kept Secret of the Ancient World," *Field Artillery Journal*: May-June 1981, 54-57.

Anna Komnene, *The Alexiad*, from Fordham University's Medieval Sourcebook, https://sourcebooks.fordham.edu/basis/annacomnena-alexiad00.asp

Alex Roland, "Secrecy, Technology, and War: Greek Fire and the Defense of Byzantium, 678-1204," *Technology and Culture*, Vol. 33, No. 4 (Oct. 1992), pp. 655-679

The Chronicles of Theophanus the Confessor, trans. Cyril Mango, Clarendon Press, Oxford, 1997.

Easter Island

Whitney Dangerfield, "The Mystery of Easter Island," Smithsonian Magazine, March 31, 2007.

Frontiers. "Solving the Easter Island population puzzle." ScienceDaily.

ScienceDaily, 20 September 2017. <www.sciencedaily.com/releases/2017/09/170920100100.htm>

Georgia Lee, "Feast and Famine: A Gourmet's Guide to Rapa Nui," *Rapa Nui Journal*, Vol. 18 (2) October 2004.

PBS online, NOVA, "Secrets of Easter Island," November 2000, https://www.pbs.org/wgbh/nova/easter/civilization/giants.html

William Reville, "What's the story behind the mystery of Easter Island? It's not set in stone," *Irish Times*, Jan 21, 2021.

THE GREEN CHILDREN OF WOOLPIT

Ben Johnson, "The Green Children of Woolpit," *Historic UK*, https://www.historic-uk.com/CultureUK/The-Green-Children-of-Woolpit/

Michal Madej, "The Story About the Green Children of Woolpit According to the Medieval Chronicles of William of Newburgh and Ralph of Coggeshall," *Res Historica*, 49, 2020, 117-132.

GENGHIS KHAN

Sh. Bira, "The Mongols and their state in the twelfth to the thirteenth century," UNESCO Silk Roads Programme, https://en.unesco.org/silkroad/knowledge-bank/mongols-and-their-state-twelfth-thirteenth-century

Charles Q. Choi, "The story you heard about Genghis Khan's death is probably all wrong," LiveScience, July 27, 2022.

Erin Craig, "Why Genghis Khan's tomb can't be found," *BBC Travel*, July 19, 2017.

National Geographic: Education, "The Pax Mongolica," https://education.nationalgeographic.org/resource/pax-mongolica/

Abigail Tucker, "Genghis Khan's Treasures," *Smithsonian Magazine*, March 24, 2009.

Wenpeng You, et.al., "Genghis Khan's death (AD 1227): An unsolvable riddle or simple a pandemic disease?" *International Journal of Infectious Diseases*, volume 104, p 347-348, March 1, 2021.

CAHOKIA

Lee Bay, "Lost Cities #8: Mystery of Cahokia - Why did North America's largest city vanish?" *The Guardian*, August 17, 2016.

Thomas E. Emerson, et. al., "Paradigms Lost: Reconfiguring Cahokia's Mound 72 Beaded Burial." *American Antiquities*, Vol. 81 No. 3 (July 2016), p 405-425.

David Nield, "The Mystery Deepens over Why the Lost City of Cahokia was Abandoned," *Science Alert*, April 17, 2021.

Diana Yates, "Fresh look at burials, mass graves, tells a new story of Cahokia," Illinois News Bureau, Aug 4, 2016, https://news.illinois.edu/view/6367/391694#image-4

ALICE KYTELER

Mrs. J.C.J. Murphy, "Alice Kyteler," *Kilkenny Archeological Society*, https://kilkennyarchaeologicalsociety.ie/wp-content/uploads/2020/12/OKR1953-09-Claire-Murphy-Alice-Kyteler.pdf

St. John D. Seymour, *Irish Witchcraft and Demonology*, 1913.

Bernadette Williams, "The Sorcery Trial of Alice Kyteler," *History Ireland*, Issue 4 (Winter 1994), Volume 2.

MACHU PICCHU

Mark Adams, "Discover 10 secrets of Machu Picchu," *National Geographic*, November   6,   2018 https://www.nationalgeographic.com/travel/article/secrets

Robert J. Gangewere, "Machu Picchu: Unveiling the Mystery of the Incas," *Carnegie Online*, Carnegie Museums of Pittsburgh, September/October 2003, https://carnegiemuseums.org/magazine-archive/2003/se-poct/feature1.html

Kelly Hearn and Jason Golomb, "Machu Picchu 101," *National Geographic*, https://www.nationalgeographic.com/history/article/machu-picchu-mystery

THE PRINCES IN THE TOWER

Ethan Bale, "The enduring mystery of the Princes in the Tower," *Historia*, July 21, 2022.

Eleanor Cracknell, "The Princes in the Tower?" Windsor Castle College of St. George Archives, May 15, 2012, https://www.stgeorges-windsor.org/the-princes-in-the-tower/

Joseph Hall, "The Grave of Richard III," Historic UK, https://www.historic-uk.com/HistoryUK/HistoryofBritain/The-Grave-of-Richard-III/

A.S. Hargreaves and R.I. MacLeod, "Did Edward V suffer from histiocytosis X?" *Journal of the Royal Medical Society*, Volume 87, February 1994, pp. 98-101.

University of Essex News, "'Research reveals DNA of the 'Princes in the Tower,'" July 11, 2018 https://www.es-sex.ac.uk/news/2018/07/11/research-reveals-dna-of-the-%E2%80%98princes-in-the-tower%E2%80%99

University of Leicester, "Richard III: Discovery and Identification," https://le.ac.uk/richard-iii

GREAT ZIMBABWE

Mawuna Koutonin, "Lost Cities #9: racism and ruins - the plundering of Great Zimbabwe," *The Guardian*, August 18, 2016.

Zeb Larson, "The Ancient Remains of Great Zimbabwe," *BBC Travel*, September 26, 2022.

Webber Ndoro, "Great Zimbabwe," *Scientific American*, January 1, 2005, https://www.scientificamerican.com/article/great-zimbabwe-2005-01/

THE DANCING PLAGUE

Maris Fessenden, "A Strange Case of Dancing Mania Struck Germany Six Centuries Ago Today," *Smithsonian Magazine*, June 24, 2016.

Daven Hiskey, "This Day in History: June 24, 1374," *Today I Found Out*, https://www.todayifoundout.com/index.php/2012/06/this-day-in-history-1374-thousands-of-people-on-the-streets-of-aachen-germany-suddenly-suffer-from-the-forgotten-plague-dance-mania/

Kallie Szczepanski, "How the Black Death Started in Asia," *ThoughtCo.*, August 11, 2019,

https://www.thoughtco.com/black-death-in-asia-bubonic-plague-195144

YASUKE THE BLACK SAMURI

Naima Mohamud, "Yasuke: the mysterious African samurai," *BBC News: Africa*, October 14, 2019, https://www.bbc.com/news/world-africa-48542673

Kat Moon, "The True Story of Yasuke, the Legendary Black Samurai Behind Netflix's New Anime Series," *Time*, April 30, 2021.

EXPLORATION

Joan Baxter, "Africa's 'Greatest Explorer,'" BBC News, December 13, 2000, http://news.bbc.co.uk/2/hi/africa/1068950.stm

Romeo H. Hristov, "The Roman Head From Tecaxic-Calixtlhuaca, Mexico: A Review Of The Evidence," https://www.unm.edu/~rhristov/calixtlahuaca.html

Eugene Lindon, "The Vikings: A Memorable Visit to America," *Smithsonian Magazine* December 2004.

The Irish Times, "Tim Severin: Writer and explorer best known for the Brendan Voyage," Jan 2, 2021, https://www.irishtimes.com/life-and-style/people/tim-severin-writer-and-explorer-best-known-for-the-brendan-voyage-1.4448332

Eric Weiner, "Coming to America: Who Was First?" *NPR Books*, October 8, 2007, https://www.npr.org/2007/10/08/15040888/coming-to-america-who-was-first

ALSO BY E.B. WHEELER

Nonfiction:

Utah Women: Pioneers, Poets & Politicians

Mysteries of the Old West

British Fiction:

Born to Treason

The Royalist's Daughter

The Haunting of Springett Hall

Wishwood (Westwood Gothic)

Moon Hollow (Westwood Gothic)

A Proper Dragon (Dragons of Mayfair 1)

An Elusive Dragon (Dragons of Mayfair 2)

A Subtle Dragon (Dragons of Mayfair 3)

Cruel Magic (Iron & Thorns 1)

Utah Fiction:

No Peace with the Dawn (with Jeffery Bateman)

Letters from the Homefront (Utah at War)

Balm for the Heart (Utah at War)

Bootleggers and Basil (in *The Pathways to the Heart*)

Blood in a Dry Town (Tenny Mateo Mystery)

A Company of Bones (Tenny Mateo Mystery)

The Bone Map

Juvenile Fiction:

Alejandra the Axolotl and the Big Mess

ACKNOWLEDGMENTS

Thank you to my critique group The Writers' Cache and to my beta readers, Alex, Dan, Karen, and Zoey, for their feedback and taking some of the mystery out of writing. And as always, I couldn't do this without the understanding, patience, and support of my family and especially my husband.

ABOUT THE AUTHOR

E.B. Wheeler attended BYU, majoring in history with an English minor, and earned graduate degrees in history and landscape architecture from Utah State University. She's the author of over a dozen books, including *The Bone Map, Utah Women: Pioneers, Poets & Politicians,* and Whitney Award winner *Cruel Magic,* as well as several short stories, magazine articles, and scripts for educational programs. The League of Utah Writers named her the Writer of the Year in 2016. In addition to writing, she consults about historic preservation and teaches history. She's always been fascinated by King Arthur and the Middle Ages and hopes to someday find Camelot (so hopefully it's real).

www.ingramcontent.com/pod-product-compliance
Lightning Source LLC
Chambersburg PA
CBHW071002120626
46546CB00003B/888